WORKING WITH

Spirit Guides

WORKING WITH

Spirit Guides

how to make contact with angels, fairies and power animals

Teresa Moorey

Bounty Books

First published in Great Britain in 2008 by
Godsfield Press, a division of Octopus Publishing Group Ltd

This edition published in 2015 by Bounty Books,
a division of Octopus Publishing Group Ltd
Carmelite House
50 Victoria Embankment
London, EC4Y 0DZ
www.octopusbooks.co.uk

An Hachette UK Company
www.hachette.co.uk

ISBN 978-0-75372-933-5

A CIP catalogue record for this book is available from the British Library

Printed and bound in China

contents

INTRODUCTION

As you read this book, you will realize something wonderful – you are not alone. Around you, close by, are spirit helpers ready to give you guidance and encouragement, to protect you when you need it and to bless you. Deep in your heart you may always have known that they were there; as a child you may have experienced their presence and may even have communicated with them. They are waiting for you now, to open your inner eyes and be aware of all that they can offer you.

Spirit guides come in many different guises, each with its own special gifts and messages. Angels may carry blessing and healing, fairies come with magic and the inspiration of a glimpse into the Otherworld, power animals bring strength and guidance while ancestors offer wisdom and serenity. Your spirit guides will probably come to you in a form with which you feel most comfortable or feel the greatest affinity, either by temperament or cultural conditioning. However, it is possible that all spirit guides are essentially the same, and simply manifest in the way we find most acceptable. Distinctions may not matter too much; what is important is the love and blessing that we receive.

Because we are generally taught that spirit guides do not really exist, the first step to contacting our guides is to begin to dismantle the walls of disbelief and scientific dogma that stand between us and the spirit realms. The first chapter is concerned with learning how to relax, since tension is the greatest barrier between us and other dimensions. Understanding meditation and how to be active on the astral plane is another step, along with beginning to notice signs of the guides working in practical ways in daily life. Simple ritual is also explored, as this is a beautiful and effective way to raise consciousness.

The following chapters introduce angels, fairies, power animals and ancestors, looking at their specific gifts and characteristics, the traditions associated with them (where appropriate) and ways of drawing closer to them and making contact. There are many practical suggestions, since it is important to remember that being 'spiritual' does not have to entail detaching from this world. Rather, it may involve becoming more vividly aware of the beauties and gifts of this world. Crystals and essential oils can all help this process. In addition, there are meditation exercises to practise when you truly wish to journey into another world – the world of your guides.

Contacting your guides is part of realizing that there is so much more to existence than we generally assume. It is uplifting and it can be fun; laughter is a fitting companion to reverence and spirit guides often have a wonderful sense of humour! Open yourself to the joy that is all around you and as you walk through life, do so in the knowledge that powerful and benevolent beings walk beside you.

Teresa Moorey

Keeping a note of all your experiences and feelings can keep your mind focused on your spiritual guides.

LEARNING TO APPROACH YOUR SPIRIT GUIDES

This chapter paves the way for you to make contact with your guide and to gain some understanding of what spirit guides are all about. We will be looking at how guides operate and what kind of communication you may expect to have with them. Making a link with your guide is a question of becoming attuned to signs of their presence, and these may come in subtle ways, or through apparently very ordinary circumstances. Becoming receptive allows us to see that apparent coincidences have important meanings and are connected with the workings of our guides.

Spirit guides have different levels and different functions. Power animals and some types of fairies are generally closer to the material world than angels and Ascended Masters (a spiritually enlightened being who has evolved through spiritual transformation), but this does not mean that animals and fairies are inferior. What your guide or guides have to offer will be explored, along with the role of crystals, oils and other props that can attune you to the beauties of the world and help change your state of mind. Perhaps the most important skill that you can learn when attempting any spiritual development is the ability to relax. You will be taken through a step-by-step exercise to dissolve tension. Having mastered this, you can then embark on the guided visualization that will help to connect you to your guide on the inner planes.

Meeting your guide is rarely a matter of dazzling visions and explosive revelations – rather it is a gradual and joyful dawning of the realization that guides are there.

what are spirit guides?

Life is much more than a series of bleak and empty experiences bounded by a void at either end. Instead, it is a journey where we evolve, find meanings and a connection with the cosmos. Spirit guides help to remind us that this world is but a dream and that our true home is elsewhere. However, they realize that it is this Earth and this life that we must deal with, and so they can be of considerable practical help. We may have been taught that only through suffering can we progress, but our guides help us to see that most suffering is created by ourselves and that life can be simple and joyful.

Spirit guides may come from different cultures, but usually we feel an instant affinity and connection with them.

Spirit guides are non-judgemental and non-denominational. Your guide will come to you in a way that is recognizable to you, but that doesn't mean your guide is truly that particular manifestation. For instance, if you are from a Christian background, you may feel an affinity with angels, whereas a nature-worshipper might see an 'angelic' being as a landscape *deva*, which is a type of fairy. For the purposes of this book, the generic term 'spirit guide' is used for any helpful entity, not just for the more transcendent Ascended Masters, to which the term is often applied. Guides may be understood as pure energy, but it is much easier for humans to relate to something they recognize. Rest assured, your guide wants you to be aware of his or her presence. If you try to make contact, your guide will know you are doing this and will, in turn, reach out to you.

no rights or wrongs

When consulting spirit guides, we may want concrete answers, but that is not the way things work! Truth is like a jewel – it has many faces and there is no one right way, but many ways. In fact, the word 'right' may be misleading; unless we are malevolent or destructive, there are no wrong choices – just learning opportunities. The

Sometimes a guide may have a connection that comes from a past incarnation or different culture – such as a Hindu deva.

analytical psychologist Carl Jung (1875–1961) wrote that a problem is never resolved at the level on which it was created. Our guides may show us how to shift perspectives and to become more complete, and part of the journey may be to realize that our problems are not truly relevant. Above all, we need to let go of the damaging 'shoulds' and 'oughts'. Often we can have the best of both worlds if we can open ourselves to the love that is around us and understand that sensuality is a gift and life is a celebration.

Our spirit guides are there to empower us, not to smooth everything out on our path through life. We are responsible for our own actions and our own karma, which is cause and effect, not punishment, and links us to the cosmic pattern. Although a true spirit guide is deeply wise and far-seeing, he or she does not know everything – the future is largely our own to create, and with the help of our guides it can be a joyful one.

noticing signs of your guide

Most of us go through life unaware of the spirit world, and even those of us who know it is there behave as if it wasn't most of the time. As a consequence, guides can rarely communicate directly, at least at first. After all, there is no point waving your arms at someone who is wearing a blindfold!

The exercises in this book are designed to help you take off the blindfold, at least for a while. However, initially, it may help to think about any experiences you have had that might indicate you were being watched and guided by a spirit presence. For instance, if you have ever been at the point of utter despair you may have felt, as I have, a wonderful sense of peace and contentment, coming as if from nowhere.

a feathered friend

Sometimes a guide may show him/herself in small ways — the trick is to notice their presence and be guided by them.

Once, when I was a teenager and going through worse traumas than most people of that age, I went into my room in a state of anxiety and misery to find a white dove sitting on my bed! The bird had obviously come in through the open window, but when I switched on the light, instead of panicking it remained quite still. After a few seconds it simply flew back out of the window. In my dark state of mind, my initial interpretation of this event was morbid. But I remember that after this visitation, my mood lifted, I felt comforted and slept peacefully in the bed where the dove had rested. I have since realized that the dove was one of my guides doing his best to reach out to me in a way that I could not mistake.

angel in a van

A friend, who regularly works on the subtle planes, had an experience of a rather different kind. While driving through town on her way to a meeting she became hopelessly lost. She pulled over to the side of the road, and while trying to calm herself down, a white van drew up. A man got out, came over to her and asked her if she was lost. She said she was and he replied that he was going the same way she was headed and she could follow him! Grateful and relieved, she did so, and his white van led her through the rabbit warren of streets. Her destination reached, he drove off with a wave. Later she realized that she had been helped by an angel and was amused that such celestial beings can manifest with a strong regional accent!

Not all such encounters are so dramatic or noticeable, however. Much of the help is small – we find a parking space, run into someone we need to meet, find something that helps us. Sometimes it seems that there is a voice whispering to us, an inexplicable fragrance in the air or a special gleam where the sun catches a raindrop. All these may be the start of contact with your guide. Keep your eyes and heart open.

Open your heart to the peace and blessing around you – they may be signs of your spirit guide trying to make a connection with you.

the role of crystals and essential oils

Many exercises in this book involve the use of crystals, essential oils and other substances. The important messages from these gifts of nature is that life is sacred and that the spiritual is all around us. Crystals and incense can help you change consciousness, so that you may more readily draw close to your guides.

crystal energies

Many people believe that crystals are alive and home to special 'energies' that can provide a channel for spiritual power. Some also believe that they are inhabited by spirit beings. Traditionally, different crystals are reputed to have specific properties, although almost all have therapeutic and 'lucky' qualities. Specific crystals will be mentioned in the relevant sections of this book, but the most important point to remember is that it is always your own response to a crystal that is of greatest significance. Often it will seem that a crystal 'calls' to you, and you should heed that call, rather than advice from any book.

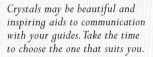

Crystals may be beautiful and inspiring aids to communication with your guides. Take the time to choose the one that suits you.

choosing crystals

When choosing a crystal, listen to your body and intuition. Many crystals are easily and inexpensively obtained as tumble-stones, but larger crystals as balls, pyramids or clusters can be stunningly beautiful and uplifting.

It is best to cleanse any newly acquired crystals, since they can absorb energies from their surroundings. Leave the crystal overnight in a bowl of organic rice or rose petals (throw the rice or petals away afterwards), pass them through the smoke of a lavender joss-stick, or simply visualize them being washed clean by pure water.

Essential oils and fragrances help to open your mind and lift your mood, creating a suitable atmosphere for spiritual journeys.

'Charge' your crystal by holding it between your palms and sending your vital force into it, imagining it pulsating with your energy. Store crystals for ritual use wrapped in black velvet or if you want to leave special crystals on display, re-cleanse them regularly.

using essential oils

Essential oils are concentrated essences extracted from plants (wood, flower, leaf or seed), and are usually sold in small glass bottles. Try to buy pure essential oils from a supplier you trust. They can be heated in a diffuser to release their scent, or diluted for massage in a carrier oil such as grapeseed oil – two drops per 5 ml teaspoon.

Essential oils seem to carry the magical secrets of nature and, as scent, have the power to change consciousness by their effect on the reptilian brain stem – the most instinctual part of us. For this reason they are very useful in rituals. Essential oils should be treated with respect since they are potent and can cause allergy or damage to skin or furniture. Most oils must be diluted in a carrier oil and some have contra-indications for children and pregnant women. Consult an authoritative guide before using them on your skin, and do not ever ingest them. Store all essential oils in a cool, dark place. Joss sticks may also be used for fragrance, but their origin is more doubtful. Again, go with what feels right for you.

drawing close to your guide

Ritual should be beautiful, enjoyable and uplifting. It helps us to change our consciousness, and an effective ritual provides a powerful suggestion to the subconscious mind that shifts are taking place. The following simple ritual is designed to help you open yourself to communications from the spirit world. It is intended to detach you somewhat from your daily life and ordinary ways of looking at reality so that you may become aware that your guide is close by.

The main purpose of this ritual is to cleanse. This is certainly not because you need to be 'purged' in any way, or because you need to be somehow 'made worthy', but because you need to be able to leave our cultural constructs behind in order to be free to explore. However, it is also a good idea to be cleansed a little of modern life, which is exceptionally polluted and complex.

pre-ritual preparations

If you are a patient person, you may like to prepare for a month beforehand, but if that seems too long, then try to give yourself a week. Of course, if you work in an office bashing away at a keyboard and come home to boisterous children, all of this will be a tall order, but do your best! During this preparation time try to:

- *Drink at least 2 litres (3½ pints) of spring water per day.*

- *Eat mainly fruit and vegetables.*

- *Avoid meat, especially non-organic meat.*

- *Keep to organic, local foods as far as possible.*

- *Get plenty of sleep – seven hours a night is a good basis.*

- *Avoid stress as far as you can.*

- *Get as much fresh air as possible.*

- *Keep a journal about your feelings.*

- *Keep television viewing and use of computers and mobile phones to a minimum.*

- *Avoid contact with disruptive people.*

preparations on the day

On the day appointed for your ritual, arrange to be alone and undisturbed. Disconnect the phone, turn off your mobile phone and do not turn on the TV, radio or a computer. If you have not been able to avoid stress and contact with challenging people in your lead-up time, do at least make sure that you don't encounter any of these on the day.

Start the day by taking a long walk, either alone or with a dog – not with a human, even your best friend! Try to think only positive thoughts; make sure you have a nice daydream with which to distract yourself; keep that uplifted feeling.

On your return, take a leisurely bath or shower using luxury oils if you wish. You should also have a treat or two lined up – a special new fragrance, silky garment or a cream tea – since contact with your guide is pleasurable and life-affirming. The sensual is a sacred gift to be honoured, and this time is special.

A bath can always be a small ritual in itself – don't miss the chance to alter your mental state in this way.

drawing closer ritual

You will need two white candles, some lavender oil and a picture of an archway, gateway, doorway or path that appeals to you. An amethyst geode will form a wonderful 'gateway' to the Otherworld if you can obtain one. Lavender oil is very gentle and can be placed neat on the skin, although it is always best to do a patch test on your wrist 24 hours before applying, in case of allergy. If you wish, you can be naked for this part of the ritual or wear comfortable clothing. Make quite sure you won't be disturbed.

1 Prop up the picture you have chosen between the two white candles and light them. Take the lavender oil and anoint yourself: first on the feet, saying 'may my feet walk upon a blessed path', then on your knees, saying 'may I kneel only before what is truly sacred'. Anoint yourself just above your pubic area, saying 'may I create what is true and beautiful', and close to your heart with the words 'may my heart be full of love'. Finally, anoint your forehead, saying 'may my mind be free and the doors of perception opened'.

2 Turn now towards your picture. Imagine that you are walking through the gateway or down the path, leaving your old life behind and going into something bright and new. Simply go into this space and stand still – do not progress further at this stage.

3 Find yourself in a pleasant place where greenery flourishes and birds sing. Look about you and take it in with all your senses.

4 Tell your spirit guide in any words that come to you that you are making a change in your life and that from now on you are going to try to be as aware as possible of the communications and workings of your guide. Speak of your hopes and fears if you wish, and ask for guidance. Do not try too hard to be aware of answers – your guide may make contact with you in ways you do not expect, and if you are concentrating on one way, you may close off your mind. Avoid trying to force the issue or expecting too much too quickly. This is a life-time journey.

5 When you feel your ritual is complete, thank your guide, even if you have not been particularly aware of any presence. When you think about all of this later, you may realize that something did happen, but because it was not what you were expecting it escaped your notice. Extinguish the candles and celebrate by eating and drinking something delicious – now may be the time for cakes! Eating will help to close down your spiritual centres and is an affirmation of life.

6 You have now embarked on a fresh path – the path of growing awareness of your guide, who will be with you every step of the way. Make notes about your experiences and feelings in a special journal (see pages 20–21) and congratulate yourself on having taken an important step.

daily drawing closer activities

There are a number of daily activities you can undertake that will help you draw closer to your guide. Keeping a journal, setting aside time to be on your own to reflect and to tune into yourself will help, as will collecting the tokens you feel that your guide has left as a mark of his or her presence in your life.

keeping a journal

Get in the habit of recording any thoughts, feelings or experiences about your guide. Note meaningful coincidences and unusual happenings as well as anything more dramatic such as 'flashes' of cognition. Write down anything that springs to mind; later on you may see that it is significant. As you write, imagine that your guide is standing beside you, reading what you have written.

quiet time

However busy you are, take some time each day to relax, detach and remind yourself about what is really important. During such times you may be more able to attune to your guide. Set aside five or ten minutes a day when you can 'talk' to your guide; you can do this aloud if you wish or just in your head — your guide will hear anyway. Make this a habit and your mind will become 'programmed' with the idea that at certain times this communication is going to take place.

Making time to concentrate on your guides is a way of honouring them and sends powerful messages to your subconscious.

ask for advice

Get in the habit of inwardly consulting your guide whenever you have a decision to make or at times when you feel troubled and in need of advice. Don't expect a specific answer; just talk as you would to a friend. In time you will be aware of responses.

creating an altar

Set aside a special place to keep any tokens that you feel may have come from your guide or represent him or her. For instance, you may find a flower dropped on your path or a feather clinging to your clothing (feathers are especially associated with angels). This space may later become your altar to your guide, as explained in subsequent chapters. You can place crystals and artefacts here, and scent your space with fragrant oils, as explored in the following section.

Anything that you feel is right, such as crystal jewellery, will help you draw closer to your guides, so follow your heart.

small rituals

There are myriad small ways to draw closer to your guide. Wear jewellery that you feel has a connection with your guide – an appropriate crystal is an inspiring choice. As soon as you wake up, make a note in your journal of the dreams you remember – your guide may well communicate with you in dreams. Before you go to sleep each night, say a few words about your day to your guide and ask her or him to be with you as you sleep.

Light a candle each day as a sign to your guide that you are developing your awareness and trying to open channels of communications. And spend some time each day in a park, your garden or the countryside, or looking at clouds or stars. The natural world is a step closer to that of the spirits. Keep faith and be patient!

relaxation techniques

Learning to relax is important not just for your health but also because it is a necessary skill if you are to shift your consciousness in order to make contact with your guide. Your guide may be able to contact you when you are tense, but it is much easier to tune into other levels of being and to perform visualizations if you are relaxed.

All children require routine and your subconscious is like a child learning by repetition. Develop a routine of practising relaxation, preferably at the same time each day, to get the message into your subconscious. A daily ten minutes is much better than an hour or two at weekends. Disconnect the phone and resolve to ignore the doorbell. Pets should be excluded and people who live with you informed and asked to leave you alone. Lie down on your bed to practise, for you will naturally associate that with deep relaxation. Once you have mastered the art, then it may be best to move to a chair, rather than fall deeply asleep, which could be counter-productive!

mind/body relaxation

The simple act of relaxation will inevitably open your mind and change your consciousness. Mind and body are so closely linked that a change in one inevitably brings about a change in the other. It may be easier to change consciousness by relaxing your body rather than simply trying to extend your awareness. Practising relaxation is important for the visualization and meditation exercises, and you should always go through your relaxation routine before starting them.

As you practise relaxation in your quest for your guide, you will realize that you are already being granted a gift — that of detaching from the world and leaving all its stresses and strains behind.

technique I

1 When you are settled, bring your awareness into your body. Are there any areas of tension? Try to relax them.
2 Imagine warm water flowing over you, starting at the crown of your head, down over the back of your neck, shoulders, arms, hands and fingers, chest and back, stomach and pelvis and down your legs to your ankles, heels, feet and toes. Do this several times.
3 If thoughts come into your mind, do not fight them. Instead, imagine they are butterflies fluttering in and out, or images flickering across a TV screen. Keep in mind that you are concentrating on your body and its comfort and keep forgiving yourself if you get distracted and tense up.

technique II

An alternative method is to tense each muscle as far as you can, then let it go limp. Start at your toes and work up your body, tensing and releasing your muscles. This releases chemicals in the body that are helpful; however, some people get cramp when they do this, so be careful. Or you could imagine that your limbs are powered by little men who are dropping their tools and walking out. Experiment with ways that work for you.

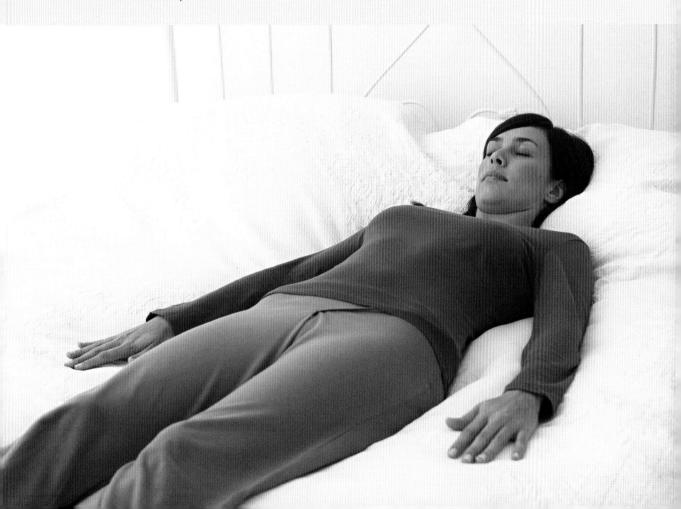

drawing closer visualization

Visualization is a way of exploring inner landscapes — it is far more than 'just' imagination, as wisdom may be born here.

This visualization is intended as an initial journey into the territory of your guide or guides, since it may be too soon to meet any spirit being. In any case, if you are not used to inward journeys, it is a good idea to get used to coming in and out of this state and feeling sure of your ground before making any contact.

a visualization into the territory of your guide

Before you begin, you might like to record the script of this visualization on a tape or CD, so that while you are relaxing you will be able to listen to it play rather than refer back to these instructions.

1 Start your visualization by relaxing completely (see pages 22–23). Imagine that you are facing the doorway that formed part of your preliminary ritual. Go through this opening and notice all your surroundings. They may be different from your earlier experience or the same, but it will be a place of beauty. Notice all that you see, hear, smell, taste and feel.

2 Walk slowly along the path, taking note of wildlife and plants that you see around you. The path follows many twists and turns, progressing uphill, and you cannot be sure where you are going. Sometimes the way is dark and shadowed by tall trees or rocks. Journey onwards.

3 The way clears and you climb onto a vast plateau. The sky is clear and in front of you lies a large, beautiful lake, reflecting the blue of the sky. Between you and the lake is a lush green meadow, sprinkled with wild flowers. A sweet fragrance fills the air.

4 As you look over the waters of the lake you see beyond it, veiled in a silvery mist, another country where glistening crystal towers reach high into the sky. A rainbow arches over the lake, forming a bridge between your meadow and the distant land. Where it touches the ground on your side, all that is close to it shimmers.

The astral planes may be very like this world, only more vivid. It is there that your guides await your presence.

5 Simply stand here and allow yourself to become acquainted with it. See the rocks, caves, trees, flowers and the gently lapping waters of the lake. Feel the sun on your face and the tender breeze in your hair. This is your place, your inward access point to the spiritual planes, and where you will build your astral temple. Here you will meet your guides who may come to you from over the rainbow bridge or from the surrounding countryside. (Do not attempt to cross this bridge, since such a journey is too advanced at this stage.)

6 Remain here for as long as feels comfortable. Do not expect to make any contact at this stage, although if you do meet your guides, consider it a bonus.

7 When you are ready, return by the path along which you came and go back through the original opening. Bring yourself back to everyday awareness by patting your body all over, eating and drinking something and writing your experiences in your journal. Congratulate yourself on your journey to the subtle planes.

safety in the spirit world

Not infrequently, people issue warnings about the dangers of the 'occult'. However, 'occult' simply means 'hidden', and so all religions deal with what is essentially occult. Many people are simply afraid of what they do not understand; belief systems that include concepts of hell and demons may encourage a view of other realms as places fraught with peril. But human beings were made to explore, and there are few safer territories than our own inner pathways to the astral planes.

Keeping fit and healthy is far from 'unspiritual' — your body is your temple and looking after it makes you strong.

Nonetheless, the astral planes do contain dangers: unpleasant entities can delight in causing trouble; and also the sheer glamour of this experience can cause some people to get carried away. So it is wise to take certain precautions when beginning to expand your awareness. Here are some pointers:

remain grounded

This world may be just a dream but it is what we have to work with, so honour its needs and those of your body, since it is the temple of your soul. Maintain sensible habits, eat well, take exercise, rest properly, laugh and have fun, do creative and practical things such as cooking to balance your abstract activities, and choose your companions with care.

keep the details private

Do not share your experiences of the subtle planes with anyone, especially the details of your astral temple. The exception to this may be if you are working in a group with a trusted leader, but still consult your instincts before saying too much and feel free to keep your own counsel if that feels right to you.

protective light

When you commence your inner journeys, surround yourself with a cloak of light, complete with hood. Imagine this as clearly as you can. Affirm that it strongly protects you.

know your guide

Choose a special sign that you share with your guide, that proves your guide is who he or she purports to be. This 'sign' may be a symbol, a word, a tune, a colour or maybe a fragrance. When you meet your guide, ask her or him to display this sign three times. Three is a sacred number, and any mischievous or malevolent presence will not be able to maintain a pretence.

A true guide will never frighten you or even intrude upon you uninvited. A true guide will not tell you what to do and will certainly never use words like 'should' or 'ought'. Nor will a true guide tell you your 'fortune' since that would take away your free will, and in any case it is doubtful that your guide (or anyone else) can see the whole of your future mapped out. Instead, a guide will give you good advice that enables you to see things from a wider angle or on a different level. As you get to know your guide, you will immediately know when she or he is present, and your guide will keep you safe.

It is important to protect yourself when you travel on the astral planes. A cloak of protective light will help to keep you safe.

building an astral temple

The purpose of building an astral temple is to enable you to better affirm your presence on the astral planes. It is a good exercise in concentration, keeping your awareness at the level it needs to maintain for contact with your guides. It serves as a strong, safe base where you may meet with your guides, and also as a place to store any token, such as a book, flower or jewel, given to you by your guide. If a guide should give you such a gift, you will generally find that it also comes to you by 'ordinary' means on the physical plane, but an astral repository strengthens the effect.

a word about visualization

This book contains a number of visualizations and this can be daunting for people who may feel that they cannot 'visualize' and so can't do inward journeys. However, visualization in this context is not necessarily about the visual. If you find it almost impossible to 'see' with your mind's eye, then imagine you can hear, smell, taste or feel your surroundings, use props such as pictures to help you and simply affirm that what you are imagining is there! Find a way to work with your own particular mindset.

astral temple tips

For the purposes of these exercises, the best place to build your temple is on the meadow in sight of the rainbow bridge. Your 'temple' does not have to be imposing, or even look like a temple in the usual sense. Here are some pointers:

- When you think 'astral temple', what is the first image that comes to mind? This may be a good starting point.
- Your astral temple can resemble a building that is familiar to you in the everyday world. There are advantages to this because it makes it easier to construct.
- Your temple should represent safety, peace and beauty to you, but it can also be cosy and rustic.
- Your temple might not be a building – it could be a grove of trees, a stone circle or even a boat.

how to build your temple

1 Before beginning to build your astral temple, prepare yourself by relaxing as explained earlier (see pages 22–23) and proceed as for the drawing closer visualization (see pages 24–25).

2 When you get to the meadow with the rainbow bridge, choose the spot for your temple and begin to 'build' it. You may picture this being done practically (for example, if it is a brick building, it may be built brick by brick), or you can visualize it in totality, immediately, becoming more solid as you 'flesh it out'.

3 Concentrate for as long as feels comfortable, then leave and return down the path to your archway, bringing yourself back to the everyday world as explained earlier.

4 When you revisit, your temple may seem less substantial than when you left it, but as time goes by it will become more solid and permanent.

5 Once you have built the outside, enter it and complete its interior in as much detail as you like, making it your spiritual 'home'.

6 Repeat this inward journey every day for a week or longer if necessary, strengthening your temple with each visit. Make sure there is a path from the door of the temple leading to the rainbow bridge.

The rainbow is an important image that oftens figures in myths and legends. Its symbolism can help you on your quest.

ANGELS

Perhaps the most easily recognized and widely accepted spirit guides are angels – certainly the major religions of Judaism, Islam and Christianity feature these wonderful beings as emissaries of the Divine. Spirits of other faiths may also be angelic. However, angels are non-denominational and certainly non-judgemental. When making contact with angels, it is best to leave dogmatism behind, and think instead in terms of love, acceptance and blessing, although some angels may indeed be forthright in their messages!

There are legions of angels, and in the following chapter we shall be looking at the angel hierarchies and their place in the cosmic order. 'Angel' is a generic term for all of these celestial beings, but it is also the specific name for the type of angels that are closest to humanity and this world. It is on these that we shall be concentrating, and also on the archangels. No angel is 'superior' or more holy than another; those whose work is most earthly are just as valuable as those closest to the Divine.

Angels offer healing, protection and inspiration, and we shall be looking at ways to invoke these special gifts, as well as learning how to spot signs of angelic presence and honour these wonderful creatures in ritual, meditation and by making an altar and angel cards. Your own special angel is your guardian angel, and ways of drawing closer to this being will be explored.

what are angels?

The word 'angel' derives from the Greek word *angelos* meaning 'messenger'. To humans, angels are often seen as bringers of all sorts of messages. More generally, angels in all their forms bring the 'message' of spirit into matter – they carry the blueprints of creation from the Divine into the manifest world. Like all guides, angels help us to understand that we are not alone. Through them we come to see that we are part of a living cosmos, of which we are co-creators.

Angels have long inspired beautiful works of art, bringing divine inspiration to painters and artists throughout history.

beings of pure spirit

Angels are not and never have been human; they, like fairies and nature spirits, are part of a different evolutionary pattern. They do not think or operate like us and they do not really look like us – they merely appear to us in human form (usually with wings) because that is what we understand. As beings of pure spirit they do not have form in the same way that we do. In fact, an angel can be in many different places at once, with the same intensity. However, our angels want us to be aware of them and benefit from them.

The ways we conceive of them are true and meaningful, even though they are not literal, since in our present state of consciousness we cannot perceive angels (or indeed many spirit beings) as they 'really' are. Monotheistic religions have co-opted angels as the 'good guys' in a cosmos where good and evil fight against each other, but angels do not necessarily conform to ideas of cosmic split and strife; these are human traits, and angels are beings of a love that binds all.

are angels male or female?

The answer is both or neither. Certain specific energies may be more typically male, some female, but each individual angel can manifest as either sex, mostly in accordance with the expectations of the human involved. Truly, angels are androgynous. They can make contact with us in the course of our everyday lives. Some people say that they are aspects of our soul or manifestations of the subconscious mind, but that begs questions about the nature of the 'soul' and the true extent of the subconscious. Angelic beings are as separate from us as anything else, watching over us but independent of us.

angelic records

Since the dawn of time angels have been with us in paintings and stories. In the Old Testament they brought instructions from the Almighty – the Archangel Gabriel carried news of her divine pregnancy to Mary, the mother of Jesus, and later dictated the Koran to the Prophet Muhammad. In medieval times debates about angels were lively and complex, and Renaissance artists such as Raphael (whose angelic name seems unlikely to be without significance) painted them in breathtaking beauty. Angels inspired mystics such as Emanuel Swedenborg (1688–1772), who made accurate predictions from his celestial encounters from 1747 until his death. Angels have appeared to people in situations of great danger, such as during war. A prime example is the Angel of Mons, seen by many soldiers protecting British troops at the Battle of Mons in Belgium, on 23 August 1914. At the moment, interest in angels is growing with the advance of the New Age and the development of what is believed by many to be a new consciousness in humans. Now, as never before in recorded history, ordinary people can have contact with angels and evolve as a result.

Angels are often perceived in desperate situations such as war, as they respond to the needs of humanity.

angel hierarchies

There are many different accounts presenting of the orders of angels. The most common one is that written by an anonymous theologian in the 5th century, sometimes wrongly attributed to Dionysius the Areopagite, a disciple of St Paul. In it there are three categories of angels in the cosmos, each with three subdivisions. 'Angel' is a generic term and also relates specifically to those closest to the physical. Similarly, archangel may be taken to mean any of the higher orders, but it also signifies the order just above 'angel'. It must again be noted that 'above' does not mean 'superior', since all angels are important and the physical world is a manifestation of the Divine.

orders of angelic beings

FIRST SPHERE – THE HEAVENLY COUNSELLORS

Seraphim Said to be the very highest of all the angels, they surround the seat of Divinity. Seraphim carry the music of the spheres and regulate the movements of the cosmos as conceived in the mind of God.

Cherubim These beings of light and movers of the stars, although remote from humankind, still touch our lives as their light filters down through the heavens.

Thrones These are the angels of the planets, accompanying each planet on its journey. At this point one throne is especially important to humans – the Earth Angel, who is concerned for the safety of this planet and her inhabitants.

SECOND SPHERE – THE HEAVENLY GOVERNORS

Dominions These angels regulate the activities of all the others closer to the manifest realms. They keep records, organize and distribute, and it is their task to integrate the spiritual and material realms. They follow the dictates of the Divine and are rarely directly involved with humans, although they are still relevant to our lives on Earth.

In stories angels are guides and heavenly messengers, but they may appear to us in ways that are much less obvious.

Virtues These angels have command over specific types of energy, which they are able to beam out with unimaginable power. Some people believe that we will become more aware of the virtues as humanity evolves and becomes more spiritual. As we learn to work with them, so we will progress.

Powers These angels are keepers of the history of humankind and the bearers of our conscience. They 'hold' Divine energy and dispense it in the manner most appropriate. The Angel of Death is a power, as is the Angel of Birth.

THIRD SPHERE – THE HEAVENLY MESSENGERS

Principalities The principalities serve as the guardian angels of countries, cities and large groups such as corporations, governments and multinational organizations such as the UN. They can be imagined as forces of integration. There are many of these beings involved with our planet, working towards unity, co-operation and love.

Archangels These are 'over-lighting' angels, concerned with more general areas of human activity. The archangels are familiar to humanity and preside over certain recognizable 'energy fields'. Gabriel, Michael, Uriel and Raphael are the most well known.

Angels These are the beings closest to humanity, and within this group there are many different types. Guardian angels are part of this classification; however, they do not merely 'guard' but also lead and inspire. There angels are concerned with any activity, large or small, and work to give it a positive, productive and balanced outcome.

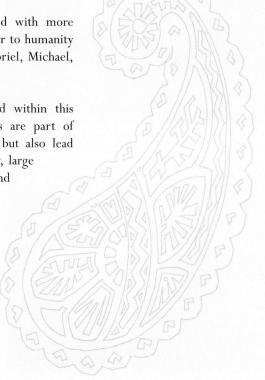

Of course, all such classifications are a human construct, a way of placing order upon the unknowable and allowing us to talk about things for which we really have no words. However, as long as you think of angelic hierarchies as a way of working with celestials, of remembering important attributes and being able to imagine these beings rather than something set in tablets of stone, the order of angels will be useful.

signs of angel visitations

Angels are all around us but we rarely credit them with the blessings they give, and even more rarely sense their presence. Becoming aware of angels isn't necessarily about being transported by a feeling of the celestial, and it is even rarer to hear the music of the spheres or see a being of light.

Like most spirit manifestations, angelic visitations can be almost ordinary, and yet you will know deep inside that something marvellous is happening. Take note and have faith in it, and gradually you will be more able to experience the truly transcendent.

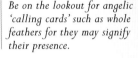

Be on the lookout for angelic 'calling cards' such as whole feathers for they may signify their presence.

Start by having an attitude of expectancy about the angels. If they are all around you, what hints are you receiving about this? How might these beings make themselves known to you? What signs might there be in this dense world of matter that angels are at work?

angel calling cards

One of the most well-known angel 'calling cards' is the white feather, and if you find one, keep it with you to reinforce your angelic connection. You might come upon a feather when you have been thinking about angels, and maybe asking for their help. It may come spontaneously, when you are feeling lost and desperate, and may follow a sensation of peace coming over you as if from nowhere. This sense of peace, calm and well-being is also a sign that an angel has brushed you with his or her wings.

other angelic signs

Look also for angels in cloud formations. There may appear to be hosts of angels over some important or sacred site. At other times, when asking for angelic support, you may see one cloud angel there just to reassure you.

Plants are sensitive and can flourish with an angelic touch. Cut flowers can last longer with the vibrancy and purity of angelic energies.

Plants may also show signs of angel visitation by flourishing beyond expectations. Cut flowers that last longer, pot plants that bloom out of season and dying plants that revive may all be evidence of angelic work, in harmony with the nature spirits, to whom they have lent their energy.

Angels are especially attuned to sound, and perhaps when you need their help, you find a friend uses the word 'angel' or you hear a song on the radio containing it. If you are very lucky, you may even feel the gentlest of touches on your shoulder, as an angel brings you comfort. Angel forms may also appear in crystals or you may come upon angel paintings or statues, just when they are most appropriate.

angel objects

Of all the forms of spirit guides, angels are the most 'socially acceptable' and because of this, there are many angel artefacts that can be purchased very easily. You may well be drawn to an ornament or piece of jewellery, not just because it is pretty but because it has angelic associations and will strengthen your ability to feel their presence. If a friend gives you an angel brooch, statue or fridge magnet, you can be sure that the angels have guided her choice. Treasure the gift all the more because of this.

calling the archangels

This section looks at 12 archangels, linking each with a sign of the zodiac. Such associations can help you to build up a 'relationship' with these beings, based on your strengths and needs. However, no association is rigid, and as you work with angels you will come to develop your own opinions. When invoking a particular archangel, light a candle in that angel's colour and hold the appropriate crystal to draw them closer.

Archangel Jophiel

Jophiel's name means 'beauty of God' and he is the bringer of sunshine, wisdom and joy. He carries the flame of intuition. His gifts include creativity and inspiration, and he dispels clouds of doubt. He increases self-esteem, self-control, courage, strength and vitality.

star sign: aries
candle colour: gold
crystal: citrine

citrine

Archangel Sandalphon

Sandalphon is an androgynous angel, depicted as a beautiful young man. He is concerned with the spirit behind earthly manifestation, is guardian of the Earth and stimulates awareness of her needs and gifts. Sandalphon brings practicality, responsibility and groundedness. With his help you can be aware of your bodily power, realizing that your body is your temple.

star sign: taurus
candle colour: brown or deep green
crystal: jade or brown jasper; smooth stone you have found

jade

Archangel Metatron

Metatron has been called the bright twin to Sandalphon's darkness. His is the light of revelation. He is versatile and makes spiritual illumination available to those who are receptive; however, his light can blind the unready, so it is advisable to approach his gifts with an open mind. He enables you to de-clutter your life so that you are free to develop.

star sign: gemini
candle colour: white
crystal: Herkimer diamond

Herkimer diamond

Archangel Gabriel

Gabriel is the archangel of the Moon. As celestial messenger, he is the angel of the Annunciation, telling Mary that she was to be the mother of Jesus. Gabriel brings the gift of fertility and builds energy by easing away physical and emotional blocks. He can help you to let go of your fears; he consoles you through loss and brings you to your spiritual home.

star sign: cancer
candle colour: orange-gold
crystal: moonstone or beryl

moonstone

Archangel Michael

Michael is a mighty archangel, commander of the heavenly hosts and a great warrior. He is often shown slaying a dragon, which means he takes on the power of this fiery beast. He is a powerful protector and dispeller of darkness. His gifts are faith and the ability to speak from your own truth. He strengthens the heart physically and emotionally. His colours are sunny yellow for strength and faith, and blue for truth and detachment.

star sign: leo
candle colour: bright yellow, sapphire blue
crystal: amber, topaz and sapphire

sapphire

Archangel Raphael

Raphael is the divine physician, bringing healing in all its forms to those who need it. He leads the guardian angels and takes care of travellers. Raphael provides support to those in the healing professions, giving knowledge, wisdom and therapeutic skill. He can also help you to heal yourself and feel a connection with nature. His is a soothing, calming presence, taking away physical and mental headaches. To invoke Raphael, place a caduceus on your altar.

star sign: virgo
candle colour: vibrant green
crystal: emerald or green tourmaline

green tourmaline

rose quartz

Archangel Chamuel

Chamuel is the healer and balancer of all types of relationships. Chamuel enables the heart to open. He encourages you to value yourself, realize what you have to offer and be positive. If a relationship is ruptured or a job lost, Chamuel brings consolation and the realization that you still have much to offer and your love has not been wasted. He can connect you with your soul mate.

star sign: libra
candle colour: gentle pink
crystal: rose quartz

garnet

Archangel Raziel

Raziel means 'secret of God' and he is lord of the mysteries of life. Things that cannot be understood by the intellect can be comprehended by the spirit, which is awakened by Raziel. The insights of this archangel can be life-changing and hard to explain to others, but they bring transformation. Raziel's gifts include self-awareness and the ability to let go of obsessions, finding inner peace and harmony. Intellectual 'chatter' gives way to true knowing.

star sign: scorpio
candle colour: indigo
crystal: garnet or electric blue obsidian

amethyst

Archangel Zadkiel

This angel teaches trust in the Universe. He brings mercy and kindness, and is called 'the holy one'. Zadkiel stopped Moses from sacrificing his son Isaac, and for this reason he may be depicted holding a dagger. He aids meditation and brings psychic protection along with a boost to the immune system. This angel removes emotions that have held you back and makes you see the bigger picture.

star sign: sagittarius
candle colour: violet
crystal: amethyst

Archangel Haniel

Haniel is a protective angel, bringing determination and the energy to see your life-mission through to its correct conclusion. He can help you to overcome the greatest negativity and to receive communication from the higher planes. His gift is the development of true individuality, independent of the expectations and pressures of others. He soothes panic and aids communication.

star sign: capricorn
candle colour: turquoise
crystal: turquoise

turquoise

Archangel Uriel

Uriel means 'fire of God' and he is linked with lightning, thunder and sudden happenings. He may be depicted carrying a scroll that contains revelations about your path in life. Uriel is dynamic, dispels fear and stimulates physical desires. His gifts are stamina, action and dynamism. Call on Uriel if you feel truly desperate, rejected or depleted and he will help you back on your feet.

star sign: aquarius
candle colour: ruby red
crystal: carnelian or red jasper

red jasper

Archangel Tzaphkiel

Tzaphkiel is best understood as a feminine presence, close to Sophia, the mind of God. She is a wonderful nurturer and brings mystical states, altered consciousness and the blessings of an open heart. She reveals other realities and the mysteries of creation. She can help you to let go of the thoughts, feelings and pressures that come from others, and brings the deepest emotional healing while releasing tension.

star sign: pisces
candle colour: lilac
crystal: labradorite or purple fluorite

purple fluorite

contacting your guardian angel

Your guardian angel is with you at all times and is more accessible than the archangels. She or he knows all your joys and sorrows and sends love of the purest kind your way, lighting your darkest hour and showing you the path to true fulfilment. Your guardian angel may also be looking after other beings, but that doesn't matter since angels can give their all in more than one place at a time.

a ritual to make contact

In preparation, create a small altar on a low table by covering it with a white cloth. On it place a white candle and a crystal such as clear quartz, angelite, celestite, selenite, or any crystal that you feel has angelic connections. To raise your awareness of the higher realms, heat neroli or frankincense oil in a burner. Effigies or pictures of angels may also be placed on your altar, along with a small vase of white flowers such as roses or daisies. White feathers and a silver or gold trumpet are also suitable, along with anything that feels right. Make sure you have a notebook and pen handy.

1 Before attempting to make contact with your angel, make sure the place where you are working is free from clutter, fresh and reasonably clean. Prepare the space psychically by imagining anything negative as grey mist that is being dispelled by pure light shining from above. Sound a bell or, better still, send the pure tones of a Tibetan singing bowl ringing around your room.

2 Light your candle and sit comfortably in front of your altar with a straight back. Allow your body to relax. Remind yourself of safety in the spirit world on pages 26–27 and don your cloak of light as described there. Affirm that you are going to make contact with your angel and ask for his or her presence.

3 Close your eyes and imagine that you are climbing seven white, mist-shrouded steps. When you reach the top step you are above the mist, bathed in wonderful light. Allow yourself to feel open and welcoming and ask your angel to come to you. Be patient and remain serene and relaxed. Soon you will feel peace and joy, and many other sensations that are special to you, as your angel draws close.

4 Ask the name of your angel and converse for a while. If you cannot make contact with your angel this time, stop your meditation after about ten minutes. Do not lose heart – you can try again another day. If you truly want to contact your angel, you will.

5 When the time feels right, thank your angel, say goodbye and go back down the seven steps, counting down from seven to one, and reunite with your body. Place your palms flat on the floor to ground yourself and have a sip of water. Note down all you have experienced in your notebook.

an angel healing ritual

Once you feel connected to angels, you will be able to work with them to direct positive intentions. Sending healing is one of the most gratifying ways to do this, but it is important to take the right approach. Firstly, you should visualize the person you are healing as being well, not 'getting better'. Secondly, it is unwise to focus on specific physical results, as you cannot be sure what you are doing. It is always best to gain the consent of the sick person before doing any healing ritual. However, sending the purest love can only be of benefit.

Raphael is the archangel most associated with healing, so set up a working altar to him. You will need an emerald candle, some eucalyptus oil and if possible an emerald green cloth to cover your working area. If you have a picture or statue of Raphael, place this on the altar. Raphael is often depicted with a pilgrim's staff, a caduceus, a bowl, a fish and a wallet, so place these on your altar also, if it helps.

healing ritual

Before doing your ritual, meditate for a while. Let yourself relax and be aware of all the love there is in the Universe. Let your mind dwell on all that is positive and wonderful. Ask Raphael to draw near and help you with his healing power. Imagine the wondrous presence of this archangel – tall and radiant, clad in vibrant green. Be aware of his love and the beauty of his presence.

1 Rub eucalyptus oil into the candle and light it. Gaze at the flame and imagine it growing into a sphere, about the size of a football. Hold out your hands and imagine that you are holding this sphere. Feel the love in your heart overflow and enter the sphere – your hands will get warmer as you do this. Ask Raphael to lend his power to the sphere. Imagine the mighty archangel extending his hand and sending his holy light into the sphere.

2 When you feel ready, 'throw' the sphere roughly in the direction of the person to be healed. (It doesn't matter if you get this wrong or if the person is a long way away – the sphere will still find its destination.)

3 Imagine the sphere of light bursting over the patient, showering them with wonderful emerald radiance, and imagine them smiling and vigorous. When this is complete, place your palms on the ground and let yourself return to the here-and-now. Thank Raphael for his help.

4 You can repeat this exercise as often as you feel able. Usually it will uplift you and give you more energy, but if it depletes you, then you may be opening yourself up too much, so don your cloak of light before you start, relax and do not be too intense.

5 You can also 'charge up' a piece of jade, peridot, chrysoprase or emerald by directing the energy-sphere into the stone. This makes a wonderful gift to someone who is not feeling well.

your angel altar

- Cinnamon – Jophiel
- Patchouli – Sandalphon
- Lavender – Metatron
- Jasmine – Gabriel
- Frankincense – Michael
- Chamomile – Raphael
- Ylang ylang – Chamuel
- Neroli – Raziel
- Cedarwood – Zadkiel
- Pine – Haniel
- Clove – Uriel
- Clary sage – Tzaphkiel

Setting up a permanent altar in your home is a positive and practical affirmation that you are bringing angels and their influence into your daily life. Your altar can be a shelf, a cupboard top or any convenient surface that allows you to place objects there safely. Tend your altar regularly, thinking about what is on it and using it to commemorate any angelic encounters that you have.

angelic colours and fabrics

Initially, cover your altar with a pure white silk or cotton cloth – natural fabrics are best. When you feel you have made contact with one of the archangels, place a smaller cloth of the appropriate colour over the white one to mark this, if you wish. Do the same if you want to draw the energies of a particular archangel into your life. Check pages 38–41 for colours, crystals and artefacts associated with the archangel whose help you need, and keep these on your altar until you decide to change them. Let your altar serve you as a portal to the realms of the angels.

angel wings

One of the things we most associate with angels are wings, and people who are in contact with the angelic realms have wing-like energy-patterns in their aura. A pair of white wings makes an evocative centrepiece for an angel altar, and although these can be obtained from some New Age shops, you can make your own out of white paper. Angel statues are also easy to obtain, and there are beautiful ones made of crystal. If you decide to invest in one of these, choose clear quartz, which is adaptable to any angelic vibration. Crystals appropriate to any of the archangels (or just ones you like) can also be put on your altar.

The scent of Jasmine is linked to the archangel Gabriel and would be an appropriate essential oil to burn on your angel altar.

There are many beautiful and evocative images to call upon when allowing your consciousness to align with the angels.

angelic objects

White candles are an obvious choice for your altar and these can be changed for coloured ones as desired, perhaps to contact a particular archangel (see pages 38–41) or because you may sense a particular colour is appropriate for your guardian angel. Place on your altar anything you feel is an angelic 'gift' – something that you find, feel drawn to buy or have been given by a friend. Your angel card for the day (see pages 50–51) can also be placed here. Angel pictures are readily obtained and you may like to collect suitable pictures for each of the archangels, to alternate as required. A bell or Tibetan singing bowl are also wonderful additions to your altar, allowing you to cleanse and refine the atmosphere by the power of sound.

angels and crystals

Because of their special nature, all crystals may serve as a link with angels. Some specific crystals are associated with particular archangels (see pages 38–41), and when you feel a close connection with your guardian angel, you may feel drawn to a crystal that reflects his or her gifts.

However, several crystals are considered to have an especially powerful connection with the angels in general. These are a good choice for you to use on your altar since they can help to harmonize you with angelic vibrations.

angelite

Not surprisingly, this is an 'angel stone'. It is usually pale blue, with veins of white that are reminiscent of feathers on angels' wings. This crystal brings peace and a wish to care for others. It can also help you to meditate while keeping you grounded. This stone protects, but also helps you to send out healing energies to those in need. Tranquil and compassionate, it takes away emotional pain and the cruelty that can come from this. Generally, it lifts the mind and opens the way to angelic inspiration.

Take your time when attuning to crystals. Each has a different characteristic and may be able to help you in its own special way.

celestite

This crystal is a forerunner to angelite, into which it transmutes after millennia of compression. Celestite is transparent, generally blue but sometimes with red or yellow tinges. It creates balance and attracts good fortune, clears the mind and opens you to new experiences. Celestite is especially good for creativity, bringing wonderful ideas seemingly from nowhere – it fosters the alignment of the intellect with the intuition. If you wish to recall your dreams, keep celestite close to your bed and place it on your forehead when you awaken. Celestite can stimulate clairvoyant abilities and bring angelic communication.

celestite

danburite

A rarified crystal that quickly aligns the heart to the angelic realms, danburite is generally pink or lilac, and also yellow or white. This stone can help you to see your path in life clearly and enable you to feel uplifted. With the influence of this stone it is possible to move beyond the effects of past traumas and to see things in a different and more celestial light. Danburite also helps in lucid dreaming in which you may meet your angels consciously. It is a helpful friend during any changes in life.

rutile quartz

This smoky stone has strands of gold, brown or red that are like angel hair, which is why it has also been called angel hair quartz. This is an energizing stone that enables you to see obstacles for what they are, to overcome fears and phobias and to move forwards spiritually. Placed on your altar, rutile quartz will stimulate you to make the necessary changes in your life to facilitate contact with angels.

rutile quartz

blue topaz

This beautiful healing stone fosters forgiveness and generosity, making you aware of your own gifts. It enables you to recognize the patterns by which you are living, and the unconscious beliefs that shape your world; these may have nothing to do with your true path in life. It connects you to the angels who can enable you to find your truth and be wise.

making angel cards

A wonderful way to tune in to the angelic realms is to make your own angel cards. As you work they will help to boost your intuition, enable you to make contact with your angelic helpers (including your guardian angel) and generally improve your life.

You can approach making the cards in a variety of ways; before starting you may like to meditate on the subject, perhaps by making an inward journey to your astral temple (see pages 28–29). Once there, you can ask the angels to visit you and bring you some ideas of the gifts they have to offer and that you need. You may wish to do this several times. Always make a note of what you have learned after each meditation.

which angel?

The list of archangels found on pages 38–41 is a sound basis for your angel cards. You may wish to research other archangels or you may prefer to concentrate on angelic attributes. A list of ideas might include: love, friendship, affluence, tolerance, generosity, abundance, beauty, creativity, blessing or healing. Add others as they occur to you.

making your cards

You will need some cardboard and coloured pens, glue, sequins, coloured foil, metallic stars, glitter or anything else you like to embellish your cards. They can be as simple or as ornate as you wish. Use a set of playing cards as a template to cut your cards to size.

Dedicate each card to a different angel or angelic attribute. Decorate the card on one side, leaving the other side blank. Your decoration should express the characteristics of each angel – a card for Raphael could be decorated with green, with pictures of trees or herbs and a caduceus. If your cards are based on angelic attributes rather than an angelic being, paste on them anything that feels right. For instance, a peace card might portray a dove, abundance can be symbolized by fruit, and so on. Try to make your cards all the same size so they are easy to handle and pick out.

Making angel cards is a fun and relaxing way to draw closer to the angels — they love to see you smile and being joyful!

using your cards

Keep your cards safely, wrapped in some dark blue velvet or in a special box. Consecrate them by burning some frankincense oil, holding them between your palms and asking the angels to bless them. Imagine that your guardian angel is near and that a shaft of golden light is issuing from his or her outstretched palm and going into your cards. Thank the angels for their blessing.

Set aside ten minutes each day, when you can be quiet, to pick a card. Spread the cards out, face downwards and pick a card at random. Allow yourself time to attune to its energies. Your card can be placed on your angel altar or carried with you to inspire you. If you have time, this is a lovely way to start your day, but if evening is best, place the card beside your bed and see what dreams come to you.

the kabbalistic cross

This is a powerful ritual used to invoke angelic protection. It also cleanses, uplifts and brings peace and balance. Before you begin, however, revise the relaxation exercise outlined on pages 22–23 and also practise forming pentagrams (five-pointed stars) as described below, so that your movements flow when you actually do the ritual.

This ritual may seem complex at first, but it is just a matter of learning the way to form the pentagrams. Draw a large picture of a pentagram as a reminder, if you need to, and keep it with you along with these instructions. After practising a few times you will perform it easily.

performing the ritual

For your ritual you will need a clear quartz wand (you may use your finger if you wish, but the quartz will help to focus your mind), a red candle, a lavender joss stick, a flat stone and a bowl of water. Wear loose cotton clothing if possible – white is an excellent choice of colour, with its sense of purity.

1 Make sure that you will not be disturbed and set out your working area. Place the stone in the north, the joss stick in the east, the candle in the south and the bowl of water in the west. In this way you are placing the four elements, air, fire, earth and water, in the quarters usually associated with them in the northern hemisphere. If you are in the southern hemisphere, it is better to place fire in the north and earth in the south, since fire belongs in the direction of the sun.

2 Make sure that you have plenty of room to move and work in the centre of the elemental representations; 2 m (7 ft) should be sufficient. Light your candle and the joss stick, and pick up your quartz wand. Hold it close to your heart while you affirm your respect for all of creation and ask for the help of the angels.

3 Face north and point your crystal at arm's length into the air. Slowly describe a circle in the air around you, imagining a golden light issuing from the end of the wand. When your circle is complete, make sure that your area is spiritually cleansed by imagining impurities as grey clouds. Sweep these away with motions of your hands and face north again.

4 Turn to the east, point your quartz wand ahead of you and be aware of light issuing from its tip. Form a pentagram in the air, starting with the far right apex, going straight across to the left, down to the right, up to the top, down to the left, up to the right, finishing by repeating the initial leftwards stroke. Imagine a flaming pentagram suspended, shining above you. Say: 'I invoke the powers of air to be with me and aid me.'

5 Turn to the south, start at the top apex and form the first stroke of the pentagram down to the right, up to the left, across to the right, down to the left, up to the top and finally down to the right again. Say: 'I invoke the powers of fire to be with me and aid me.'

6 Now turn to the west, start with the left apex and form the first stroke of the pentagram, proceed to the right, down to the left, up to the top, down to the right, and so on. Say 'I invoke the powers of water to be with me and aid me.'

7 Turn again to the north, starting with the top apex of the pentagram, moving down to the left this time, up to the right, across to the left, down to the right, up to the apex and once more down to the left, repeating your initial stroke. As you do this say: 'I invoke the powers of earth, to be with me and aid me.' Finish off by thanking the elements for being present. You are now surrounded by four scintillating pentagrams.

8 Place your quartz wand on the stone and turn to the east. Imagine the Sun is rising, bathing you in celestial light and that you are growing taller, so that your head is among the stars and the Earth a dot at your feet. Raising your hands towards the dawn, touch the tips of your forefingers and thumbs together, so your hands form a triangle. Imagine that you are catching the light of the dawn with your outstretched hands.

9 Guide your hands down to your forehead, intoning 'Atoh' (thou art). Lower your hands to your lower abdomen, directing the light towards the Earth as you intone 'Malkuth' (the Kingdom). Move your hands to your right shoulder, directing the light to the right saying 'Ve Geburah' (the Power) Now similarly to the left shoulder with the words 'Ve Gedulah' (the Glory) Finally, bring your hands to your chest, saying 'Le Olahm' (Forever).

10 Now say: 'Before me Raphael, behind me Gabriel, to my right Michael, to my left Uriel. About me flame the pentagrams and in the column shines the six-rayed star.' Extending your hands again in a triangle, repeat the cross ritual, starting with 'Atoh'. After 'Le Olahm', this time say: 'For the ages upon ages, may all be blessed!'

11 Touch your palms to the floor to ground the energy. Reflect for a while, if you wish. Thank the archangels for being present and ask them for their protection or any other gift that you need. When you are ready, take up your quartz wand, face east, thank the element for being present and form a pentagram with your wand, this time starting with the left apex and reversing the motion that you made when you invoked it. Do the same in the south, the west and the north, each time starting your pentagram with the reverse of the motion you used to invoke. When this is complete, place your quartz wand at your heart and absorb the energies of your circle.

12 Bring yourself back to everyday reality, ground yourself by drinking some water and patting your body, blow out your candle and write down your experiences in your special notebook.

FAIRIES

There are many stories in folklore about strange beings of field and forest, mountain and moor, mist-clothed lake and shimmering fountain. Fairies are reputed to help in mills and mines, and around the houses of favoured humans. Some are attached to a specific place or element (such as fire, earth, air or water), while others are majestic and bewitchingly beautiful. Fairy tales speak of marriage between mortals and elves, crocks of gold, and sometimes of abduction and trickery. Always, fairies are magical and Otherworldly.

Who are these beings? Of course, some people say they are nothing more than a flight of fancy, but they can never have sat beside a moon-pearled lake at midnight or dozed near a summer flowerbed. Fairies are many and varied beings, and while not all may be totally well-disposed towards humans (and who could blame them?), the fairies we shall be considering can all act as wonderful guides and helpers if we take the time and trouble to attune to them.

The best way to understand fairies is as nature spirits and we will look at spirits of place, elemental spirits and also the much more powerful old pagan gods, since these are the same as the fairy kings and queens of folklore. We will also consider how best to attune and communicate with these enchanting sprites so as to benefit from their guidance. Fairies are all around — hear them, feel them, catch glimpses of them from the corner of your eye and become entranced.

becoming aware of the fair folk

In folklore, fairies were often referred to euphemistically as the 'fair folk' or the 'good people' so as not to offend them, but here they are called 'fair' because their presence brings loveliness. Not all fairies are beautiful and some – earth spirits particularly – are not necessarily pretty by human standards and can have a heavy 'vibe'. However, fairies come with love and vibrancy. They are the very breath of life and without them the natural world would have no essence. In fact, it would not exist, since fairies form the energy-fields that enable the physical world to 'be' and to grow.

If you are a sensitive person with a true love of nature, you will have sensed the presence of fairies many times when out in your garden or walking in the woods. It is rare to see a fairy, and people who experience this are not actually receiving impressions with their eyes. Instead, their brains are translating what they are sensing into appropriate visual images. Not everyone does this, but if you are not able to 'see' fairies, that does not mean that you are unaware of them and cannot communicate with them.

fairy help

Fairies may be involved in many aspects of human life; however, the term fairy is not applicable to the kind of spirit who will be your personal spirit guide through life, such as a guardian angel, for instance. Instead, fairies help with specific tasks and activities, and in so doing may indeed work very closely with you for a long period, such as when you are creating something artistic or musical, or if you are involved in gardening or cooking. There are spirit beings giving form and energy to all things, from love-making to running a business, but these are perhaps better termed *devas*, from the Hindu word meaning good spirit, in order to differentiate them somewhat from the nature spirits of folklore. However, in essence they are similar.

getting in touch

The first step towards making contact with nature spirits is to relax physically (see pages 22–23). Of course, if you are walking or sitting in a park or garden you will not be able to relax fully, but be aware of your body and let tension and anxiety leave you. Now how are you feeling? How is the place making you feel? If there were beings close by, what would they be doing, what would they look like, how might they sound? You are almost certain to experience something, such as joy, excitement or a flood of energy, and this is your first contact with a fairy. Anything you feel or sense will be significant – try not to judge or analyse. Simply experience.

The fairies will notice that you are moving into their reality, but they will probably not take it very seriously. We are in their 'reality' often – when we daydream, when creativity is flowing, when we are in love – but we do not realize this and may dismiss our feelings as 'just imagination'. Imagination isn't 'just' anything – it is the most creative force we have and everything we do exists initially in the imagination.

make a fairy gift

The natural world is the most magical place of all. Take long walks and allow yourself to attune to the fairy presences.

However, fairies are not imaginary in any sense of the word; they are as real as the book you are holding, although they inhabit a different dimension and have a different vibrational rate. In order to convince the fairies that you are tuning in to them, attract their attention by 'making' them something pretty with your imagination. Hold out your hands and imagine that cradled in them is a shining, shimmering crystal, scintillating enough for a fairy gift, and offer this to the fairies. Or imagine there is a bright star over your head or that you hold a fantastic flower in colours brighter than you have ever seen. This will make the fairies realize that you are serious in your intention to make contact. After this, see what happens.

ask for fairy help

Get into the habit of acknowledging the presence of fairies and asking for their help. For instance, if you are making a cake, be aware that the cake-making *deva* is close by, and ask for help in baking something delicious. Once you do this, in all sincerity, you will become aware that there is a spiritual dimension to what you are doing and that there is a 'shape' and even a sacredness in it. You will then become aware of being helped, probably by being drawn to behave in a certain way, but it is possible that you will hear a voice or even 'see' the fairy. Similarly, if you are gardening, ask the fairies for help, since there are many spirits involved with the soil and specific plants as well as some that actually inspire what you do. You will be surrounded by a sensation of love and vibrancy. If you are engaged in something that is more subtle (although no more creative) such as playing the guitar or sketching, ask that your fairy muse empower you and you will feel lifted to another level. Certainly you will know that you do not work alone.

Performing routine tasks in a spirit of reverence turns them into a meaningful ritual and may break down barriers between the worlds.

offer thanks

Whenever you sense the fairies, and especially when you are aware that they have helped you with your tasks, always thank them. It is a good idea to get into the habit of doing things that convey thanks. For instance, if you have cooked a special meal, save just a little bit to offer to the fairies. You may leave this out on a saucer (the fairies will take the 'essence' not the physical food) or scatter it on the earth. When you cut flowers or vegetables, always leave behind a little and say a special 'thank you' to the fairy involved. You can use gestures that are meaningful to you to convey thanks – for instance, when I pick herbs I always form a pentagram (a five-point star) with my finger over the plant. Simply saying 'thanks' in your heart is enough, but physical action sets up a flow of energy and may produce better results.

Once you get into the habit of these activities, your connection with fairy guides will grow and develop in a way that may be personal to you. You are now beginning to work with your fairy guides.

fire fairies

There are four elements in the Western tradition – fire, air, water and earth – which correspond to four different states of matter: energy/transmutation, gas, liquid and solid. They also correspond to four human states of consciousness: inspiration, thought, feeling and practicality. There are spirits associated with each element – fire is the most unpredictable and also the least in evidence in these days of central heating and microwaves.

Dragons are fire spirits that represent the power of nature. Thought of as destructive, myths were created about slaying them.

Fire spirits are found in nature when it is hot – the molten core of the Earth and the seething hearts of volcanoes are home to fire fairies. These spirits may be called salamanders, although they are not all like reptiles in shape. Fire fairies dance, sparkle and crackle with an electrifying energy, and of all the elementals they are the least interested in human affairs. Nonetheless, the fire fairies have gifts that we need if we are to be dynamic.

Many fire fairies move about quickly, attracted to any flame, tending and energizing it. They are present in metabolic activity, supporting the process of converting food to energy. As humans, we have our personal salamander who empowers our muscular activity and our passions, including sexual ones. However cold the winter, fire spirits are always close, since they absorb solar energy to sustain them and are ready to burst into action whenever a flame is ignited.

agents of change

Fire fairies bring many gifts, including courage, vision and idealism. All passions are enhanced by them, and they are agents of transmutation and regeneration. They expand awareness and call forth our inner spiritual fires, so that we can see beyond present conditions into an eternal perspective; they are also associated with death and reincarnation. Fire fairies show that while the material body may die, the spirit endures.

A simple token can keep you connected to the fairies — let it be a little secret just between them and you!

finding fire fairies

You can encounter fire fairies most easily in a bonfire or an open hearth. See salamanders coiling within the heart of the flames and watch others dance and crackle in the sparks. Look deep within, become relaxed and ask to be shown the true nature of fire. You will become aware of the most electrifying energy. If you do not have access to a proper fire, lighting a candle can serve the same purpose, and it may be a good idea to light several red or orange candles at the same time.

If you need courage or energy to meet a challenge, if you want to increase your sexual powers or be especially creative, or if you have to move on in life and make changes, ask the fire fairies for their help. Light candles or a fire, invite them to draw near and imagine their energy transferring itself to you. Tie a red ribbon around your wrist as a testimony — you can wear this ribbon when you need to access the extra energy. Thank the fire spirits and promise to honour them by putting your heart and soul into your endeavours and really stirring things up!

air fairies

These spirits of the air are the very embodiment of the breeze. They work to keep the atmosphere in balance and order cloud formations. Air fairies are called sylphs – they are light and ethereal, although their size varies enormously, from great storm fairies to tiny Tinkerbell type sprites. Because they are so mobile they support angels in their tasks, and may even act as temporary guardians to humans. Sylphs are found everywhere and because they have no attachment to static life to bind them, they may cover vast distances.

Boreas, an air fairy, comes with the harsh blast of the snowy wastes, but also with wisdom. Call on him for certainty and security.

making contact

Sylphs are best contacted in high, open spaces where breezes blow freely. To draw close to these beings, go to the top of a hill where you are not likely to be disturbed and make yourself comfortable. Let your body relax as much as possible, look out at the horizon and let your heart be lifted. Now become aware of the breeze against your skin. How does this touch make you feel? What thoughts are coming into your mind? Be aware also of the sounds around you, for sound is very much a sylph medium. Can you hear whispers, sighs or songs? Take note of all you experience. If you think that the sylphs have been close by, thank them for their presence.

sylph gifts

The gifts of the sylphs include clear thought, memory, freedom, communication and music. These fairies can also aid telepathy and clairaudience, and help you to understand how your mind functions. More than this, they open the way to knowledge of your spiritual path. These gentle beings love to help in healing and creativity. They are very likely to communicate with you by a voice that you hear inside your head – if you are lucky enough to experience this, note it well.

seeking sylph guidance

You may need the guidance of the sylphs if you have an important exam or a journey to undertake, if you have to give a speech or if you are doing anything that requires clear, swift thought and self-expression. If you are a musician, especially one involved with woodwind instruments, the sylphs can help.

To make contact with your own special sylph, acquire a dream-catcher. This is a Native American artefact, usually hoop-shaped with dangling feathers, designed to 'catch' bad dreams and protect you while you sleep. It can be adapted to attract sylphs, although they can never be caught, since they are the essence of liberty itself. Get a new dream-catcher for this exercise and affirm that it is for a positive purpose. Attach an extra feather to its base and hang it by an open window. When you see it begin to stir in the breeze, ask for your own special sylph to draw near. When you are aware of the breath of your sylph stirring the dream-catcher, ask for the specific help you want, thank the sylph for being present and then detach your extra feather to take with you when you face the challenge. It is a symbol of the inspiration of your sylph.

A dream-catcher can be adapted to contact air fairies — it is a delicate and beautiful reminder of subtle sylph presences.

water fairies

Water is the source of all life. Our bodies and the Earth herself are 70 per cent water, and the developing baby floats in the amniotic sac, surrounded by water. Water also represents change – in many myths crossing a stream signifies a shift in consciousness, and baptism is a rite of passage. Water is mysterious, moody and changeable. Water fairies embody all of these attributes and many of them are hauntingly beautiful.

Water fairies, or undines, are found wherever there is water – tiny sprites dance in waterfalls, mermaids ride the ocean waves, strange and lovely beings inhabit inland waterways and magical creatures dwell in lakes and ponds. Water can be a tricky medium, for nobody knows what lies within its depths. However, water spirits are generally friendly to humans, although they may be very shy.

The water fairy Melusine can teach us how to recover our lost powers of healing, wisdom, sensuality and freedom.

contacting water fairies

To contact the water fairies, find a stretch of water where you can be quiet and peaceful – a lake may be best. Go there at dawn or dusk, when you know there will be no one else around, and bring some rose petals with you. Sit quietly and relax. Look at the water and open your awareness so you feel its atmosphere and essence. Your emotions may change and memories of the past may come to you. Take note of any impressions you have. Gently toss the rose petals on to the surface of the water, to attract the undines, and they will betray their presence in gentle ripples. Thank them for being there. If you repeat this at regular intervals, the undines will begin to trust you and may reveal themselves.

healing gifts

Undines possess the gift of physical and emotional healing, as they can wash away hurts from the past. They can also connect you to the wellsprings of your own feelings, bringing sympathy, empathy and the bonds of human love. They act as guardians to springs and wells and also to humans who honour them.

Water has the power to hold memories and feelings. Be aware of the characteristics of the water you are drinking.

If you are feeling raw or buffeted by life, if you feel lonely, sad or uncared for, you need the blessing of the undines. If you are going into a situation where you are likely to feel any or all of these emotions, or if you need emotional strength for anything, then the blessing of the undines would be most helpful. If you have a natural spring close by, you can literally 'bottle' some water spirit enchantment by taking a clean, empty bottle (preferably glass) to the spring. Ask the undines to give you some of their magic. Fill your bottle at the stream and give thanks. If there is no spring nearby, fill a bottle with bought spring water and take it to your nearest stream. Let a few drops fall into the flowing waters and ask the undines to bless your remaining water, filling it with healing powers. Decant some of your energized water into a smaller bottle and take it with you to sip, for extra strength, when you do what needs to be done.

earth fairies

Earth spirits are the power of the earth herself, from her fertile depths to the tips of the green leaves on the tallest tree. They carry the wisdom of soil and root, the riches hidden within mines, the mysterious darkness of caves and the everyday magic of things that grow, blossom, fruit and decay. They hold the knowledge of all that needs to be done in order for the earth to bring forth life, from hard work to skill, timing and patience.

Pan is an ancient god, or spirit, of shepherds and pasture. His name means 'all', suggesting that he embodies the forces of the earth.

Earth fairies are found wherever there are plants, but they also inhabit caves and mines. They guard and cherish all that comes from the earth, including crystals. Although different crystals may be associated with many other fairies, it is the special task of the earth fairies to grow and treasure them. The general name for earth fairies is gnomes, and they have a 'heavier' presence than other fairies, although those associated with flowers are much lighter and brighter.

contacting earth fairies

Gnomes are among the easiest of fairies to sense since their presence is almost tangible. Sit quietly in your garden and you will become aware of them at work all around you, catching their movements out of the corner of your eye. Walk through woodland in a relaxed and open frame of mind and you will see them dancing in a haze of green around each tree-trunk. A different type of earth fairy can be found in caves, and their presence can be oppressive and make you uneasy. However, they mean no harm to humans, although they may be somewhat resentful at first. Bring the gnomes an offering of a coin or jewellery, and thank them for all their work.

gnomish gifts

Earth spirits can be very useful since they embody practicality and common sense, the ability to handle and acquire money and knowledge of how to grow things. They are very protective, but also have an intense energy that can be empowering when you need to work hard and mobilize all your powers of endurance.

If you have a gruelling practical task ahead of you, if you have job or money worries or have need of a special skill, ask the gnomes for help. Go to a place where you feel close to the gnomes, and ask that they be present. Tell them that you value all the hard work they do for the earth, for crops, flowers and trees, and thank them. Tell them you need help, support and protection, and ask them to give you a special stone to empower you. Remember that all stones are precious to the gnomes, who value and honour Mother Earth. If they have heard your plea, you will find that your eye lights upon a specific stone. Pick up your stone, treasure it and promise that you will give a gift to the earth in return, such as planting a flower or clearing rubble. Take your stone with you when you need extra strength and touch it in challenging moments for a boost of gnome-power!

Tap into the ancient powers of the earth and let her wisdom help you with the aid of a special stone and the blessing of the gnomes.

landscape *devas*

Sand paintings were used by the Native Americans, who were well aware of the spirits of the land and how sacred it was.

Many fairies are concerned with the earth and with growing things, but a landscape *deva* is a greater spirit that presides over a complete locality. Such a locality may be very large, such as an entire mountain, or it may be a smaller area, such as a wood or meadow. If you open your perceptions in the ways we have explored, you will be able to sense when you are moving from the territory of one *deva* into that of another. There is usually a definite change in atmosphere.

People who hold the land to be sacred, such as the Native Americans and the Australian Aborigines, are well aware of these spirits and have traditions associated with them. The land is honoured by ritual, the wishes of the *deva* are adhered to and permission sought before any interference is made with the natural order. Some of the ills we experience as modern city-dwellers in the West are due to the fact that we do not consult the *devas* before arrogantly imposing our wishes upon the Earth. In extreme cases, building plans can go awry because of this.

contacting the *devas*

Making contact with a *deva* is rewarding in itself, allowing you to feel a part of all that lives, connected by loving bonds. Because we all become so used to our own locality, it may be easier to connect with the *deva* of somewhere less familiar. Go to a place with which you feel a resonance and let yourself relax. Open your heart and ask to make contact with the *deva* – imagine an extensive, beautiful consciousness spreading its wings over the countryside. *Deva* contact is more exalting and uplifting than contact with humbler spirits, and you may feel lifted and enlarged, surrounded by melody or light. Ask the *deva* what it wants and you may feel guided in some way, maybe to travel a certain path, clear some weeds or become involved in an environmental concern. Give thanks and leave an offering, such as some seeds or food for wild animals.

your garden *deva*

It will be helpful to contact the *deva* of your garden in order to get the best from your patch of land. It is usually best to leave part of the garden to grow wild, because that provides a strong base for the nature spirits who will give the garden life. Relax and go into your meditative 'space'. Ask the *deva* what would be best for the garden. You may get ideas about what to plant and where, and it is likely that everything will grow much better if you get into the habit of making this contact. If you are contemplating landscaping or building, always try to find out what the *deva* wants before proceeding. Better ideas than the ones you had before could well pop into your head! Try to back up thoughts with deeds, even if this is only watering the garden, and always thank the *deva* for making contact (even if you are not quite sure you have done this).

Every plot of land has its own spirit presence. Awareness of and respect for this can help a garden to flourish.

spirits of place

Spirits of place are similar to landscape *devas*, but are less tied to the natural world and may be strongly attached to human activity – there is a *deva* connected to all human endeavours. A spirit of place is often built up by a combination of human activity and the basic character of the land.

Some places have a very strong atmosphere – this is the spirit of place. You will be able to serve this and be uplifted.

Most cathedrals and many churches have a palpable spirit, because they have been lovingly and harmoniously built on land that was already highly charged by devic activity. Houses, too, have a very definite 'spirit'. Some houses are naturally more atmospheric than others, but it is possible to enhance the ambience of any dwelling by calling on and empowering the spirit of the place.

honouring your household spirits

Start by seeing your home as an entity in itself. You can do this even if you live in a semi-detached or terraced house, an apartment or even just one room. Imagine that around the boundaries of your dwelling there is an energy membrane. This membrane is the 'skin' of the spirit of place, although spirits are not, of course, so sharply defined and may move about. Nonetheless, the spirit of your home is attached to your home and will always be there if needed.

contacting your home spirit

Relax and make contact with your home spirit by expanding your consciousness. How do you feel, emotionally and physically? What comes into your mind? What is the character of your home spirit and what might it want you to do? Do not expect clear answers at first – by starting to make contact you are setting up a resonance and soon you will be instinctively attuned to your home spirit. The atmosphere in your home will become stronger and more enveloping and you will feel nurtured and protected.

Consult your home spirit before decorating or renovating. Sometimes the changes you plan will turn out not to be such good ideas, and better notions may come into your head. If so, thank your spirit for them. When you are doing household chores such as cooking and cleaning, ask the spirit of your home to be with you, to energize and inspire you. Dusting and vacuuming can be seen as acts of love and honouring towards your home spirit. Such activities can feel more meaningful and less onerous if perceived in this way. Cleanliness and freedom from clutter allow the spirit to breathe and are a statement that you value your space and the spirit that presides over it. It is also a good idea to honour your spirit of place on your fairy altar (see pages 78–79) with special crystals, flowers or other tokens. This shows gratitude and respect, and also allows you to more fully enjoy your home.

meeting elemental fairies and *devas*

Performing this visualization will enable you to connect more powerfully with the energies and essences of the elements, so that you can draw on these forces within you when you need them in life. It will also help you to open out more completely to the fairies in nature and to receive their wisdom and guidance in whatever form it comes.

visualization to meet fairies and *devas*

Before you begin, it might be helpful to record the visualization to play on a tape or CD while you are actually doing it so that you do not have to refer back to the instructions and break your mood and concentration. Prepare for this visualization by relaxing as explained on pages 22–23.

1 Begin by imagining yourself going through your door or archway and finding yourself on the path. You are going to travel to the plateau and your astral temple but you will be making some detours along the way. Walk along the path, noticing how rough and stony it is. Your way is shrouded by tall trees. Around you is a smell of soil and root – rich, cool and musty. You see a pathway on your right and you take it. Now it seems you are walking farther and farther into the woods. Strange flowers carpet the ground and fly agaric mushrooms nestle around the tree roots. Ahead of you looms a rock face, and as you approach, you see the mouth of a cave, gaping darkly.

2 Go towards this cave and sit in front of it on a flat stone. The moist scent of the cave breathes all around you, and you hear a sound of distant drumming, as if the heart of the Earth is beating. The sound grows louder and you realize that it is being made by marching feet coming closer and closer. The gnomes are coming from their dark abode to meet you. Watch and wait in an attitude of love and expectancy. What happens now is your own experience. Ask the gnomes for the gifts of common sense, practicality, worldly comfort and understanding of nature. Communicate respectfully, give thanks, pledge an offering to the Earth, such as planting flowers or herbs, give thanks and take your leave.

3 Walk back the way you came and rejoin the main path. As you continue your walk, notice that the atmosphere is becoming moist. You can hear water flowing and splashing. Take a turn to the left and find yourself walking along a new path, bounded on either side by lush greenery. The sound of splashing is getting louder. Ahead you see a shining waterfall cascading into an emerald pool. The water is the purest and loveliest you have ever seen, gleaming like silver where it courses over the rocks and deepening to wonderful shades of green, blue and purple.

Walk the paths of beauty and contact the elemental spirits in the landscapes of your mind. This is your gateway to the central plane.

4 You hear the sound of gentle laughter, which then softens to haunting singing. You know that the undines are on their way to greet you. Sit on a fallen tree trunk beside the lake and wait for them in love and wonderment. What happens now will be personal to you. Ask the undines for the gifts of understanding, love, beauty and healing. Commune with the undines, ask questions and answer them. Pledge an offering to the waters, perhaps clearing a stream or taking an offering to your local spring. Give thanks and leave.

5 Rejoin the main path and find yourself walking upwards. You are mounting towards your plateau. Up, up you go and the air becomes fresher and cooler. Soon you reach the plateau, but now you see a higher outcrop to your right, which you climb. At the top you find a vast panorama spread out beneath you, the horizon fading into a blue haze, on which white clouds are gathering. As you watch, these clouds seem to grow. Soon you see that they are forming the turrets and spires of a wonderful cloud-city that is moving towards you, borne by the winds.

6 You begin to hear whispers and the breezes play about your head. You realize that the sylphs are on their way to make contact. Stand, as the wind lifts your robes, and wait for them in love and rapture. What follows will be personal to you. Ask the sylphs for the gifts of clear thought, far sight, wisdom and peace. Speak with the sylphs, and answer their questions. Pledge an offering to the air, such as burning sweet oils. Give thanks and leave.

7 As you return to your plateau, you see that rays of the Sun, piercing through the cloud-city, have struck the earth with a particular intensity. A haze of heat is rising, strengthening, crackling until it bursts into living flame. These flames are feeding on nothing, burning nothing. They are pure energy, leaping, dancing, twisting and flaring.

After completing the visualization, burn sweet essential oils as an offering to the sylphs for their gifts from the cloud city.

8 You approach this fire expecting the heat to be unbearable, but instead it seems to welcome you and to dim its heat to a comfortable warmth. Around you sparks caper and sizzle. You realize that the salamanders are on their way to meet with you. Stand with your face towards the heat and await the salamanders with an attitude of love and excitement. What follows will be personal to you. Ask the salamanders to give you courage, to enable you to be passionate and committed to what is important to you, and to energize and inspire you. Speak with the spirits and answer their questions. Pledge to honour fire by regularly lighting a candle. Give thanks and leave.

9 Turn now towards your astral temple, walk towards it and enter it. Ask for your own particular guide to come to you – this may be a *deva*, an angel, a power animal or an ancestral spirit. Reflect with your guide on what you have just experienced. Are there any special lessons for you to learn? Which of the elements did you find it easiest to connect with, which the most difficult, and why? What might this say about your personality and avenues that you could develop? Which element do you need more or less of in order to be balanced or to achieve what you need? Ask your guide to intercede for you with the elementals, to have the gifts you need.

10 In due course, thank your guide and take respectful leave. Come back down the path and find your gateway. Return to the ordinary world, ground yourself by eating and drinking and record your experiences in your special notebook.

your fairy altar

Although similar to an angel altar, your fairy altar will have subtle differences. While fairies can certainly guide and empower you on your path through life, they are less likely to show you the path. Fairies are connected to the world of nature, and through them you can become linked to all that lives, as well as acquiring certain strengths.

getting started

Leaves and flowers on your altar will especially help you to attune to the nature spirits that have helped them to grow.

As with the angel altar (see pages 46–47), your fairy altar can be a shelf or any surface that will allow you to place objects on it. You will need candlesticks, an oil-diffuser and a small vase. As time goes by you can cover the altar with a cloth of an appropriate colour and add crystals, statues, symbols, pictures and any number of things that seem appealing. To get started, go for a walk somewhere you especially like. As you walk, ask the spirits of the place to show you a token – a stone, a leaf, a strangely shaped twig, or something else that you encounter. Try to be as relaxed and peaceful as you can during your walk so as to be strongly aware of the atmosphere.

When you get home, sit for a moment and think what the walk reminded you of. Is there a poem or a painting that comes to mind? If so, and you have this to hand, place it on your altar with your token and light a candle. Thank the fairies for being present and for bringing magic into your life. As time goes by you will be able to expand on this exercise and it will feel natural to honour the fairies on your altar after any activity that involves them.

honouring the old gods

The old pagan gods may be most easily understood as a type of fairy, which in no way trivializes them! These gods may be honoured on your fairy altar in order to bring their gifts into your life. For instance, if you want love and passion, Greek Aphrodite (Roman Venus) of the wild woodland groves can come to your aid. Burn a rose pink candle and scatter rose petals before her, asking for the gift of love. Research other gods from any pantheon, and if you don't know which flowers they prefer, go with what you feel. The short exercises for the elemental forces can also be performed with your fairy altar as a focus.

honour your household spirit

Most important of all, honour the spirit of your household on your altar. If you find a figurine or artefact that expresses how you imagine this spirit, place it there. If you have flowers or herbs growing in your garden, bring a posy. Light a candle for your household spirit whenever there is an important family occasion, and bring recipes to the altar when you are planning a special meal. When the meal is cooked, place a few morsels on your altar to say thanks. Later you can take them outside and offer the 'essence' to the fairies.

Sometimes when you are alone in a wild place you will sense the presence of the old gods who are often the Fairy King and Queen.

fairy crystals

Crystals are a wonderful choice for your fairy altar. They can also help you to connect with the elemental spirits. Emerald, green agate, malachite and peridot are all good for calling the gnomes. Aventurine, mottled jasper and citrine are loved by sylphs; amber, ruby, carnelian and garnet are salamander stones; while amethyst, aquamarine, moonstone and lapis lazuli appeal to the undines.

There is a specific crystal known as the Fairy Cross. Its true name is staurolite and it naturally crystallizes in a cruciform shape. Legend tells that it was formed from the tears of the fairies when they heard of the death of Jesus. Staurolite is a good addition to your fairy altar, but it is also a beneficial stone to carry, bringing good luck and a touch of fairy magic. It also relieves stress and enables you to balance work and play so as not to become over-wrought.

Crystals add power and magnetism to your fairy altar. Always choose what feels right to you, rather than following a book too closely.

contact through scrying

Perhaps the best way to use crystals to contact fairies is by 'scrying'. This is actually short for 'descrying', and means looking for images in a translucent object, namely the well-known crystal ball. Beryl is the traditional crystal for this, but you can use clear quartz or indeed any crystal that appeals – amethyst may be a good choice. Obtain as large a crystal as you can afford and cleanse it as explained on page 15.

1 You need to be on your own, peaceful and relaxed to scry. Perform your relaxation routine first (see pages 22–23) and light a candle on your fairy altar. Heat some lavender oil in your diffuser. Sit, holding your crystal comfortably between your palms and support your hands on your lap or on a table top. Or leave your crystal on its stand and gaze into it. Make sure the room is dark except for the candle, the flame of which should be reflected in the crystal.

2 Affirm that you are protected (see pages 26–27) and ask to see only what is good. Ask for your fairy helpers to draw close. Stare deep into the heart of the crystal and allow your mind to be peaceful. In time you will 'see' pictures, either with your physical eyes or through your 'mind's eye'. Some people find that although they are using their eyes, impressions come to them through sounds or scents.

3 Take note also of what you feel – hot or cold, joyful, comforted, peaceful. Ideas that come into your head now may be messages from the fairies. Try not to judge anything for now; simply experience.

4 If you are new to this, ten minutes will be enough time. Give thanks to the fairies and wrap your crystal in black velvet. Make a note of anything you have experienced, however odd, and in time it might show up as part of a pattern. You are inviting the fairies to communicate, and one way or another they will!

oils and herbs

There are myriad associations between growing things and fairies, but some are more powerful than others. There is a tradition of the 'fairy triad', three trees that reputedly enable you to see fairies when they grow together. These are oak, ash and hawthorn. Where you spot all three close by, sit down and allow yourself to enter a dreamy state and see what happens!

roses

Plant essences are able to communicate straight to the primitive and instinctual paths of the brain.

Roses of all types are very pleasing to the fairies, especially the Fairy Queen. Climbing dog rose is very magical, but if you want to bring the fairies closer to you, dilute two drops of rose essential oil in a teaspoon of carrier oil such as sweet almond or grapeseed, and anoint your forehead before going out for your walk. (Be careful not to get any oil in your eyes.)

other well-loved fairy flowers

Primroses are loved by the fairies, and if you want to fill your garden with the Little People, plant red and blue ones together. Foxgloves are fairy flowers and it is not a good idea to pick these. Herb Robert and red campion are also special and great to have growing in the wilderness part of the garden. Cowslips and forget-me-nots can supposedly lead you to treasure buried by the fairies, which is no doubt an allegory for being able to see the magic in life, which surely is 'buried treasure'! Thyme is another fairy herb – to dream of them place a sprig beneath your pillow, and to encounter them wear a sprig of the herb.

essential oils

Specific oils are associated with the elemental spirits, and heating oils in your diffuser will attract fairy folk, enabling you to benefit from their energies.

- Fiery salamanders are drawn to cedar, cinnamon, clove, frankincense, orange, peppermint and rosemary.

- The airy sylphs love benzoin, orange bergamot, citron, lavender, lemongrass, lily-of-the-valley, marjoram, mint, pine and sage.

- The watery undines like lemon balm, camphor, cardamom, eucalyptus, jasmine, lemon, myrrh, rose, sandalwood, spearmint, thyme and vanilla.

- There are fewer oils that please the earthy gnomes, but you can try patchouli and cypress.

If you need an influx of the energies and gifts of these spirits, try heating an appropriate oil (or experiment with combinations of oils) and burning candles of a suitable colour: red for the salamanders; white or light blue for the sylphs; purple, deep blue or green for the undines; dark green, brown or even black for the gnomes. You can also massage yourself with these oils, appropriately diluting two drops of essential oil in a teaspoon of carrier. It is a good idea to do a patch test first, to check for allergic reactions.

other uses

Fragrance is an especially potent way to summon your house spirit, and while pot pourri is considered undesirable by some Feng Shui experts as being 'dead' matter, there can be no such objection to essential oils, which are a distillation of the vibrancy of the plant. Sit quietly in your favourite spot at home and ask your household spirit which fragrance might be most suitable. A hint may come into your mind – for instance you may 'see' a plant, or you may even smell the fragrance. If not, start with what you like and take it from there.

Fragrance can change your consciousness. Take the time to develop your own approach in order to create the effect you desire.

fairy tokens

Interacting with the spirit world isn't just a matter of inward journeys and meditations. Sometimes things go better when we actually do something. Performing little rituals are ways of changing our consciousness and stopping us from being isolated in our intellectual ivory towers. Besides, the fairies like them!

daisy chains

Fairy tokens can be offerings you make to the fairies or things you create in order to draw closer to them. One well-known 'fairy token' is the daisy chain, which was believed to offer protection against fairies – a child wearing one could not be kidnapped by the Little People! However, the Daisy Fairy is very powerful and opens a connection to many good spirits of the plant world, so when you weave a daisy chain you are weaving fairy magic! Take one to your fairy altar and drape it around your effigy for a special blessing.

herbal tokens

A chaplet of thyme is considered a wonderful fairy token – make one by weaving three or four woody stems together in a circlet or bind with green thread, to fit your head. Tiny fairies were believed to live inside straw. Straw is easy to twist into any shape you like – use it to make magical shapes and fairy symbols, such as an equal-armed cross symbolizing the four elements in balance.

One traditional fairy token is the corn dolly, which is made to preserve the spirit of the corn after harvest, to guarantee that it would grow again the following year. Cutting the corn was believed to be hazardous, for the corn spirit might be angry. If you go out into a field when the grain stands tall and golden (corn is used here in the broad sense, meaning grain), you will hear the whispers of the grain, and sometimes sense the anger of the nature spirits who know that all this glorious growth is going to be mown down by humans who may not appreciate it. Ask the spirits if you may gather a few stalks from the field. Take them home and bind them in a bunch with red

Tying a piece of fabric to a tree near a special well is a time-honoured custom to ask the fairies for healing.

thread (red symbolizes life). This bunch is a simple corn dolly — if you are talented, make something more life-like. Place the dolly on your fairy altar until the coming spring, as a sign of the renewal of life.

healing well tokens

Tokens of a different sort are left at healing wells. Traditionally, people tie a piece of fabric on a tree near the well in order to ask for healing. It is best if this is a piece of organically produced cotton or lace, rather than soiled dressings, which might have been favoured in the old days! There really isn't any excuse for polluting the area with anything soiled or synthetic. If you need healing, hold your token between your palms while you ask the fairies to take away your hurt. Then bind the token on the tree, affirming that you leave behind your illness to be washed away by the fairies of the healing well.

POWER ANIMALS

Animals function as special sorts of guides, since they are strongly connected to the Earth plane. Their raw energy can make them staunch allies in daily life as well as faithful guardians and pathfinders in the astral realms. Your power animal will embody the essence, experience, wisdom and abilities of all the animals of that type, but will also be uniquely and vibrantly your own.

In relating to our power animal we need to be mindful of the respect due to all living things. Native Americans use the phrase *mitakuye oyasin*, which means 'all my relations'. Everything in the animal world and indeed the plant kingdom is related to us and must be cared for if we are to care for ourselves. This is not New Age sentimentality, but an understanding that all living things are connected and interdependent. Realizing and accepting this is important for our survival.

Power animals are part of shamanic tradition, which has its own ways of looking at the cosmos and of expressing that relatedness through rituals. Native Americans use the medicine wheel, which is a symbol of strength, since medicine means power. You will find out how to meet your power animal and also about journeying in order to find the answers to questions. Finding your power animal and bringing it more actively into your life will enable you to feel more able to meet life's challenges with strength and confidence.

shamanic tradition

Because the concept of power animals derives from shamanism, it is important to understand a little about this tradition. Shamanic practices date from a time when humans were supposedly more 'primitive', so the quality of contact with power animals is slightly different now, although certainly not less 'spiritual'.

spirit journeys

Shamen, or 'magical priests', would make spirit journeys into the Otherworld in order to pick up information that was important to the tribe, or for healing purposes – these journeys, therefore, had a definite practical purpose. Power animals provided help and protection on these journeys, and the essence of the animal was deeply entwined with that of the shaman. Anthropologists have theories about how tribal people think, but many also agree that it is impossible for us with our 21st-century mindsets to understand fully the totally different mindset of humans who live close to nature. In using power animals as part of spiritual growth and understanding, we may be using them differently from the tribal shaman. However, power animals can help us to connect with our deepest selves in a very dynamic fashion.

Most cultures have a shamanic tradition, dating from a time when the spirit world and its occupants were perceived as close by.

animism

It is probable that all cultures have a shamanic inheritance, since shamanism has its roots in animism, the belief that all is alive, which may be the earliest form of spirituality. Shamanism was not sought as a vocation, because it was far too arduous; usually the shaman was chosen by the spirits as a result of a near-death experience or other trauma. Shamanic work usually includes healing of some kind, and if you are drawn to this, then it may well be because of certain wounds that you have endured, which now serve as openings into other levels of reality.

shamanism around the world

There are shamanic traditions all around the globe. The Australian Aborigines have a culture that is 40,000 years old, which includes shamanism. South America, Mexico, the Orient and Siberia all have a shamanic history, but perhaps the best known is that of native North Americans, on whose colourful traditions we shall be calling. Shamanism is a life path, and if you decide that it is your chosen path, then you will need to explore what this means to you and where it can take you. The differences between the shamanic path and any other spiritual path are mostly ones of terminology, but the shaman's task is largely one of healing – of the planet and of other humans. There are contemporary groups and 'lodges' that you can join in order to have company on your search, although you may travel alone if you wish. The central practice of shamanism is inward journeying to the rhythmic sound of a drum, which was referred to as the 'shaman's horse'.

Whether you are interested in the practice of shamanism as such, or merely wish to connect with your power animal, try the following exercise to help you feel a closeness with nature. Native Americans call trees the 'Standing People' and this exercise is simply about hugging a tree. Of course, this is the ultimate New Age cliché, but don't let that blind you to how powerful and uplifting it can be.

drawing close to nature exercise

Trees have a special essence and they may well be more advanced on their particular evolutionary path than we humans. Take this knowledge in your heart as you walk out looking for a special tree to which you feel drawn. It will be best if you choose somewhere private, for you do not want the curious glances or the judgements of other people to interfere with your experience.

1 When you find a tree that seems to welcome you (not all do!), then go up to it, touch it, lean on it and be close to it. Close your eyes and see what comes into your mind. Do you feel the tree has something to say to you? What images, emotions or memories come to you?

2 Sit quietly under the tree for as long as you like and notice your surroundings. Note the flight of birds, the fall of leaves, patterns of sunlight and shadow, raindrops. Listen to all the sounds – as you become aware of them you will hear more and more. Smell the scents, taste the air, feel the ground beneath you. Try not to analyse.

3 After a while stand up and feel what it is like to be the tree. This is not the same as communing – it is more a partaking of the essence, which is a shamanic activity. Feel your feet turning into roots, snaking their way deep into the soil. How does it feel? Is it soft and rich or hard and dry? Or both? Your branches reach up to embrace the sky – feel the wind in them, the gentle caress of bird's feet against your twigs. Be aware that your skin is bark, hard and rough, that you do not move along the ground but stand strong upon it and within it, and deep within you the sap oozes slowly. Concentrate on being the tree, imagining all the details. Then stop imagining and just be. You are the tree.

4 When you are ready, come back to everyday awareness. Now you can interpret what has happened if you like, and analyse it as much as you want. Record your experiences in your spirit guide notebook.

The purpose of this exercise is to enable you to feel a true connection with nature. This will be personal to you, and will not necessarily be like anyone else's experience. By taking the trouble to make this 'connection', you are giving out signals that you are ready to meet your power animal and that you understand something of the world it inhabits. You are beginning to practise 'nature mysticism' – the sense that all of life is sacred and you are becoming ready to explore this further.

Trees were known as the 'Standing People' by Native Americans who respected them. A tree may act as a portal to the Otherworld.

exploring the otherworld

Shamanic tradition teaches that there are three 'worlds' in the Otherworld – Upper, Middle and Lower. This type of concept can be found in most cultures and the three worlds are often connected by a sacred river, road or a great tree, like Yggdrasil in Norse mythology. The roots of this enormous ash grow in Hel (Lowerworld), through Midgard (Middleworld), and its branches spread into Asgard (Upperworld), the realm of the gods.

The image of the three worlds can serve as a map when travelling into the Otherworld, helping us to make sense of experiences.

middleworld

Middleworld is the world we inhabit — almost! It is the world you will have entered during the exercise on pages 90–91. It is the world of nature spirits, of 'atmospheres', of whispers on the wind. It is the world you are travelling in when you start visualizing (see pages 24–25). Your journey along the path to the lake takes place in Middleworld.

lowerworld

Lowerworld is not Hell, although it may be home to some things we fear, until we have learned to recognize them for what they are. Here we may encounter spirits of the ancestors and also spirits of realities that we have repressed, so these can seem monstrous and scary. However, Lowerworld is a powerhouse of energy, and sometimes journeys there can be among the most cathartic and life-changing, because what we most fear is often our own power in disguise. However, because of our cultural background of Hell, devils and even eternal damnation, Lowerworld journeys are best not attempted until you have a strong allegiance to your power animal and hopefully a supportive group with which to discuss your experiences.

upperworld

Upperworld is the province of angelic presences, dreamed of and sought after by mystics and those who seek enlightenment. Star beings and planetary energies dwell here, along with certain deities. This is a blessed and beautiful place, but it is not essentially 'better' than the other realms, since each has its function and place. The land beyond the rainbow bridge in your initial visualization (see pages 24–25) is an Upperworld place.

Your journey will begin in Middleworld, where you meet your power animal. For the moment concentrate on this exercise. Think about a place you love in the natural world. This should be somewhere familiar that you feel drawn towards. It should have access to Lowerworld in the shape of a hollow tree, tunnel or stream that goes underground, and access to Upperworld via a tall tree or steep slope. Flesh out the scene. Once you have established this, you have your journey centre and will soon be able to start journeying.

a selection of animals

Whatever power animal guide you have will always be special to you and have its own individual meanings. However, there are some generally accepted characteristics that seem obvious with regard to animals. Hawk, for instance, is far-seeing and fox is cunning.

Of course, these qualities are established from a human perspective; as you relate to your power animal you may find it offers you some unexpected gifts. The following list is just a starting point and is composed of animals familiar to many people around the world.

FALCON
The falcon is a bird of prey, riding on the winds and scanning the Earth with laser-sharp eyes. Falcon brings courage, imagination and breadth of vision. With falcon you may find freedom and travel far.

BEAVER
Beaver is a worker and master of his environment. He teaches the importance of getting one's hands dirty and engaging with life. He can show you how to put plans into action, finish what you start and enjoy a sense of achievement.

DEER
Deer is swift and graceful. She is mistress of camouflage, alert, sensitive and poised. Deer teaches trust in one's instincts and the ability to act quickly and appropriately. She also shows the ways of love and gentleness, and how a light touch can achieve so much.

WOODPECKER
This bird clings tenaciously to trees, pecking continuously until his goal has been achieved. Sometimes he drums for sheer joy! He can show the way to build secure 'nests' for what you value and trust to the rhythms of life.

SALMON
This fish is large, very powerful and determined, finding its way upstream to spawn. Salmon brings wisdom and a strong sense of direction – even vocation – to life, finding one's true way without disturbing others.

The bear has the characteristics of strength, protectiveness and resourcefulness. She will act as the guardian of sleep and dreams.

BEAR

Bear is strong, self-protective and resourceful, hibernating through the winter to emerge with her cubs in spring. She is protective, full of common sense and sound method. She can show the mysteries of the land and acts as guardian to the land of sleep and dreams.

CROW

This bird is a powerful scavenger – raven and magpie belong to the crow family. Crow is adaptable and resourceful, looking at things first with one eye and then the other. Crow can protect your secrets and give you knowledge of the laws of nature, and what is hidden.

SNAKE

Snake brings knowledge of the cycle of transformation, through birth, sexuality, death and rebirth, inhabiting an instinctual world. Healing and wisdom are the gifts of snake, along with a wonderful sense of timing and the ability to change deeply.

OWL

This bird flies by night, seeing well in the dark, flying soundlessly, with uncanny awareness and ultra-sharp hearing. Owl brings insight and wisdom, helping you to perceive what lies below the surface and expand your consciousness.

GOOSE

The goose inhabits lonely and windswept places. She can be aggressive and determined. Her feet are on the ground but she also flies to the stars, so she brings the art of possible dreaming, renewal and achievement, purification and unexpected blessings.

OTTER

Otter is a sleek aquatic mammal, with a great sense of fun. He is a loyal mate and caring parent. His gift is joy and compassion and he encourages you to play. His message is not to take yourself too seriously, to let go and take life as it comes.

WOLF

This animal has an amazing sense of smell and a great ability to track what she wants. She can sense danger from afar and has a strong sense of pack and family. Wolf is a teacher and mentor, and excellent guide in the Otherworld, showing how to be safe, keep secrets and hunt for meanings.

The wolf as a power animal is a great mentor and can be a guide to the Otherworld, teaching you how to keep safe from dangers.

If a swan shows herself to be your power animal guide, then she will show you how to accept yourself just the way you are.

EAGLE

High-flying eagle brings the light of the soul. His gifts are intuitive flashes, spirituality and a panoramic vision. His keen sight and swiftness give him a magical quality. He will enable you to soar above everything.

MOUSE

Little mouse examines everything closely and carefully. She may seem insignificant but she spots the very thing that you need to know. She sorts, assesses and scrutinizes, and her help is invaluable if you are confused, because she will prioritize.

BUTTERFLY

It is as well to be wary of insects as totems for their energies are very different to those of humans. However, butterfly is something of an exception. Her gift is the ability to live in the 'now', to appreciate beauty and to transform, going where the winds of change carry you.

FROG

Amphibious frog is happy in more than one element. He can help you to change, making 'leaps' of understanding from one place to another. He also shows the way to wash away psychic negativity.

TURTLE

Native Americans see the turtle as representing the Earth Mother. Turtle brings groundedness, keeping the body in balance first and foremost. She brings health and shows you the way to your creative centre. (Tortoise is similar to turtle.)

HAWK

This bird is similar to eagle, far-sighted but also inviting closer, sharp-eyed inspection. Hawk reminds you to look for what you may have missed, and set your soul free.

HARE

Hares have an uncanny quality, appearing from nowhere. She shows you the Otherworld paths and the mysteries that lie there. With hare, knowledge can spring 'from nowhere' in your mind.

RABBIT

More timid than hare, rabbit encourages you to face your fears and turn weakness to strength.

HORSE
In myth, horse carries the Fairy Queen. He represents the energy within the Earth and can carry you through magical gateways.

BADGER
This creature shows how to defend your corner and stick to your guns.

SQUIRREL
Squirrel teaches preparation for the future, not just by hoarding but also by getting rid of what you don't need.

SWAN
This bird turns from ugly duckling to beauty. She teaches surrender to the flow of the cosmos and to accept yourself for the wondrous being you are.

DOLPHIN
This mammal brings the breath of life and the spirit of communication. He can show you joy and freedom.

TURKEY
This large bird brings gifts, sustenance and blessing.

BAT
Sinister and mysterious, bat inhabits the darkness. She helps you face your fears and make endings, finding your way by 'radar' to achieve rebirth.

FOX
Swift and wily, fox shows you how to remain unnoticed while you do what is necessary. He shows the value of stealth.

DOG
Dog is like wolf, showing you where you need to be loyal and committed.

CAT
Graceful and relaxed, cat also knows when to pounce! As a great hunter she teaches self-sufficiency. Fierce and sensuous, devoted mother yet fearsome predator, she shows many sides of 'female' energy.

STAG
Like deer, he is wise in the hidden ways, bringing fertility and the mysteries of nature.

The stag power animal will bring to you knowledge of the hidden ways along with his wisdom of the mysteries of nature.

journeying to meet your power animal

Journeying is another name for an inward spiritual journey, but in the shamanic tradition there are three key elements to the ritual. Firstly, it is traditionally accompanied by a drumbeat; secondly, it is performed for a specific purpose, generally to seek the answer to a question; and finally, it is not guided by a script.

Journeying is often undertaken in shamanic lodges where there is someone to beat the drum. However, if you are journeying alone, try to obtain a suitable CD in a New Age shop or similar. Avoid recordings with lyrics, for they will mislead.

seeking your power animal

1 Your first journey will be to meet your power animal. Settle yourself comfortably and relax (see pages 22–23). Find yourself in front of your archway or doorway, and go through. Put on your protective cloak and progress along the path until you come to the meadow with the rainbow bridge. Strongly affirm that you are on a journey to connect with the animal that has the abilities you most need at this time.

2 You will now see another path leading from the meadow. This path will connect you to your journey centre as identified on page 93. Walk along this path, noticing all your surroundings, sights, sounds, smells, touch, until you come to your journey centre. As you approach it you will see that it looks exactly like the place in the 'real' world, except that everything seems more vivid.

3 Once in your journey centre, ask for your power animal to come to you. Some animals are shyer than others and some come in unexpected ways. If your animal is a bird, it may come from your Upperworld entrance; if it is a frog, it may come from Lowerworld. Try to keep an open mind, and remember that the medicine of all animals is equally strong. Each has its own gifts, and even if it is not what you expect, you can learn from this and respect its powers.

4 When your animal approaches, challenge it three times with the question: 'Are you my power animal?' If the answer is 'Yes', then welcome your animal and cherish it. You may now continue to travel the subtle planes with your animal or converse with it (although it may not answer you in words). When you are ready, take affectionate leave and come back along the path to the meadow, and back to your doorway and to ordinary reality.

5 Now that you have met your animal, you can ask it to go with you on journeys, to find the answer to a question. Sometimes a different animal will come forward, and if it measures up to the challenge, this is another power animal, more suited to this journey. As you become more used to journeying, you will find new ways to use this skill. Travel well!

medicine wheel rituals

The circle is an important image that is used over and over again in esoteric practices. Among other things, it can signify eternity.

The medicine wheel is a power wheel. It is a tool for creating sacred space, for affirming a connection with the cosmos and with your power animal. It comes from the Native American tradition, but has conceptual links with the 'magic circle' used by Western occultists and encountered in the kabbalistic cross (see pages 52–53) as well as with the mandalas of Eastern traditions.

The version of the medicine wheel often used is part of the Lakota tradition, and we will look at this along with the more usual Western associations. There is no 'right' or 'wrong' version – it is about finding what is right for you. The wheel is divided into quarters, each one linked with one of the cardinal directions. Your wheel can be set out physically as an aid to meditation or a prelude to journeying, but first you need to understand how the wheel works.

examining the quarters

Most wheels are divided into quarters, and each one is linked to an element that has many other associations, such as mental abilities, colours, animals and so on. The quarters correspond to different stages in the day, the year and human life.

eastern quarter

The east is linked with the element of air. Air is about thought, mobility, communication and intellect. It is the quarter where the Sun rises, with the call to leave the domain of sleep and be conscious and aware. This is the quarter of morning, spring and youth, the entry into incarnation, beginnings, hope and promise. The colours associated with east and air are yellow and blue. Animals that have their natural place here will include birds and swift-footed animals such as deer, although many animals can 'belong' in more than one quarter or a different quarter at different times of the year.

In the northern hemisphere, the natural direction in ritual is clockwise, because that is the direction in which the Sun moves in the sky. If you live in the southern hemisphere, the Sun moves anti-clockwise, and so it is advisable to move in that direction. The meanings of south and north will also be swapped round, as the wheel is rotated through 180 degrees.

southern quarter

South is linked to midday, summer, the prime of life and the colour red. In the Western tradition it is equated with the element of fire and with intuition, passion and energy. Animals that belong in the south could be any with a red coat, fierce animals (lions, for instance) and reptiles, animals that like the heat. Because of their freedom and power, some birds may belong here too – far-seeing predators such as hawks and eagles.

western quarter

The west is equated with the element of water, which is associated with emotions, healing, memories and tribal links. The west is the place of evening, autumn and late middle age, when the personality is mellowing. Colours associated with water are greens, turquoise and purple and animals that 'belong' here are fish, dolphins, otters and similar.

northern quarter

Finally we arrive at the north, and the element of earth. In the northern hemisphere the north is the dark quarter, where Sun and Moon are never seen. It is the realm of night, midwinter, old age and death, where our bodies return to the earth and we leave this life to move on to another incarnation. Earth is linked with practicality, security and a 'hands-on' approach. Its colours are browns, some greens and some yellows (ochre), and burrowing animals or private animals such as badgers and bears belong here.

lakota differences

In the Lakota tradition, by contrast, east is fire, south is water, west is earth and north is air. East, home of sunrise, brings inspiration and its totem is the eagle. South is the place of the Moon and the tides, and its totem is the mouse, the home-maker, who notices small details. West is earth, where the Sun sinks into the ground, and its totem is the wise grizzly bear; and north is air, home of the cool winds of midnight – its totem is the buffalo, which sweeps across the plains.

making your medicine wheel

It is important for you to come to your own decision regarding your medicine wheel. Which quarter do you link with what? Which element seems most appropriate? Meditate for inspiration or travel with your power animal so you can clarify your ideas. Build up your own list of association for each quarter - elements, colours, plants, animals, scents, characteristics – anything that occurs to you. It is up to you; the important thing is that it should resonate deeply with you.

1 When you feel clear about your own wheel, set it out physically on a circular mat, coffee table or tray. Use a joss stick to represent air; a candle for fire; earth or salt in a bowl for earth; and water in a glass for water. Choose crystals, herbs, coloured threads, animal figures, postcards, ornaments – add these to your wheel. In the centre place a special paperweight, crystal or extra-thick candle.

2 Call on the directions in words of your own choosing, thinking of them as mighty spirits or animals, and asking them to be present. For instance, you might like to say: 'Spirit of the air, mighty hawk, high-flying, far-seeing, be with me today and give me your power.' When you feel that all the 'powers' of your wheel are present, let a feeling of peace flow through you, as a preparation for journeying. When you have finished, be sure to thank all the powers for being present, blow out the candles and close down respectfully.

3 You can leave your medicine wheel arranged permanently, as a kind of altar. Within it you can place an image of your power animal, wherever you feel is most helpful to you – for instance, if you need inspiration you might choose east and the elements of fire and/or air. Use your medicine wheel to affirm experiences you have had while journeying – for instance, if your power animal took you underground and you were given a jewel (which could signify creativity), place an appropriate crystal in your earth quarter. By doing this you may feel clearer about its meanings.

4 Make the medicine wheel part of your life. Create it in jewellery, on your fridge by means of fridge magnets – you could even produce medicine wheel meals! All you are doing is showing the powers of life that you are working with them and seeking balance. Let the circle be open, but unbroken.

making a medicine shield

You can make a medicine shield as a celebration of some test passed, a significant experience or wisdom gained. A good way to affirm what you have learned on an important journey is to make a medicine shield. The shield is a grounding tool and a statement.

Making a medicine shield can be an absorbing and creative task that will help you to a deeper understanding.

materials

Traditionally, a shield was made from animal skin, but many people today would find that distasteful. Canvas or felt on an embroidery hoop is good or even a circular piece of card. Shields are usually round but they can also be square or oval. Decorate it with crystals, herbs, petals, feathers, animal effigies, sequins, buttons, nuts, dried leaves, ribbons, beads, stickers — the list of what can be attached to your shield is endless.

getting started

The associations of the medicine wheel can give you a starting point to making your shield. For instance, if your power animal is hawk and you had a journey where you were inspired to take up a new course of study, the associations are with the air element, and in the case of the Western tradition wheel, with east. So your shield might include the crystal citrine, pictures of sunrise, fluffy clouds, feathers and possibly a picture representing the ivory towers of a university, wind-blown seeds or quotations from books. If you made the association with the Lakota wheel where air is north, you might prefer a midnight bird such as owl and a starry sky. As you progress, do not feel you have to be bound to anything other than your own feelings and imagination.

Always be guided primarily by your instincts when choosing a crystal and place it on your shield to represent what it means to you. Native American shields are usually pictured with feathers hanging from them, and these can be an evocative finishing touch, especially if you have an affinity with that tradition.

When your shield is completed, consecrate it in a short ceremony. Set out your medicine wheel and heat some oil of frankincense in a diffuser. Hold your shield over the wheel and ask all of the elements to bless it. Say: 'I ask for the presence of Spirit in all I do – may I be guided and blessed' or words of your choosing. Thank the elemental powers and put your shield where you can see it as you relax in order to commence journeying.

using crystals on your shield

Crystals can be particularly evocative, but you will need good glue to attach them to your shield.

- *Yellow citrine links with air and fire and brings mental sharpness.*

- *Amethyst is dreamy, wise and meditative and links with water.*

- *Red carnelian brings courage and strength and is fiery.*

- *Green stones such as jade and peridot are earthy, signifying luck on the material plane and prosperity.*

- *Agate links with air and earth and with communication.*

- *Onyx is stabilizing and earthy.*

- *Aquamarine speaks of watery emotions while moonstone is also watery and brings gifts of the Mother Goddess.*

PREVIOUSLY INCARNATED SPIRITS

In addition to the many spirit helpers we have the good fortune to be able to look to for guidance, each of us also has at least one permanent guide who was at one time human. This guide may be one of our ancestors, or, more likely, was someone with whom we had contact in a previous incarnation. Such guides have become something of a New Age cliché – they seem to be a glamorous type of figure such as a Native American, or Chinese sage. The truth of the matter is that our personal guide may very well have been such a person in a previous life, and they will reveal themselves to us in the way that is likely to be most meaningful to us. If you make true contact with such a guide, your life will be inexpressibly enriched.

Another possible type of guide is one of our own ancestors, or a relative who has passed on. There are many tales of people who have been warned of impending danger or given important messages from beyond the grave. Not everyone who dies passes immediately to a separate realm. Some remain close by, not because they are tied to Earth by a negative inability to 'let go' but because they have a calling to help someone who is left behind.

In this chapter we shall be looking at ways you can draw close to these spirits, to be discriminating about the communications you receive and grow in wisdom and joy as a result.

guides from former lives

Many people believe in reincarnation and that we meet the same people in successive incarnations as we work through karma. The word karma in this context means cause and effect, not punishment. In successive lives we are born into certain circumstances and hopefully learn and grow from these experiences until we no longer need to incarnate and work with the weighty lessons of the Earth plane. Spirit guides may be called 'Ascended Masters' (whether they are male or female) – they have left the wheel of rebirth, but are still in contact with the material plane to help others.

getting in touch

The visualization and relaxation techniques discussed in the first chapter are especially relevant to seeking this type of guide. Rituals and other activities may be helpful but they are somewhat less important, because the spirit that you are contacting is still essentially human. A smaller shift in consciousness may be required than with other guides, but this, as with all matters spiritual, is a personal thing. So be prepared to notice and record the signs of your guide, perform the preliminary ritual (see pages 16–17) and practise the daily routine, relaxation and visualization (see pages 20–25), and your awareness of your guide will expand.

The image of the Buddha is very evocative, signifying peace, wisdom and contemplation. It can serve as a focal point for meditation.

some pointers about spirit guides

- While some guides may have a generic function, if you are at the stage where you are wishing to make contact, there will be one guide who is special to you.

- Your guide knows when you are trying to make contact.

- Teaching guides tend to manifest as male, healing guides as female, but they are truly beyond gender.

- Spirit guides do not know everything. They are there to empower and clarify, comfort and support, inspire and reassure. They are not there to judge, command or control.

- Guides are fun-loving and enjoy a laugh! They are not against sensuality and pleasure.

- Questions to guides are best phrased: 'I am thinking of doing so and so. What might be the positives and negatives of this course of action?' rather than: 'What should I do now?'.

- False guidance is possible. If you follow the instructions on safety (see pages 26–27), mischievous entities are unlikely to take over, but it is still possible to misinterpret your guide, especially at first, so always use intelligent judgement and common sense, as well as your psychic sense.

Whatever wonderful experiences you may have had with angels, fairies or power animals, the companionship of your guide is the most constant blessing. If you now wish to turn your attention to making this contact, allow yourself to relax and ask yourself what your guide might look like. Ask him or her to show herself to you and see what comes to mind. Have you always felt drawn to an Egyptian image? Or to Chinese wisdom? This could be more than glamour – it could be the first sense of your guide. Light a single candle to affirm the opening of your spirit.

Lighting a candle can change the atmosphere in a room and encourage you to detach from your everyday life.

ancestor traditions

Honouring ancestors is part of most traditions; it is less about regarding them as more knowledgeable and far more about respecting our roots. Individuals who have died are not necessarily wiser, since the dead can cut themselves off from the light by their preconceptions. However, contacting the ancestors means accessing our species, wisdom and also opening the way to those of our forbears who have true guidance to offer.

an ancient practice

Ancestor worship is the oldest organized religion in China. States were governed by hereditary rulers and the ancestral temple was a vital centre for worship. Ancestral tablets are still erected in special halls or even in a household shrine. They are considered almost sacred and some people believe they hold the spirit of the ancestor.

The Romans had a tradition of honouring the *Lar Familiaris*, which may be regarded as a household fairy but was also the ancestral spirit, usually that of the founder of the family. The Lar's shrine was the hearth, and monthly offerings of garlands on the hearth were made, together with daily libations of food, wine and milk. Similarly, the *Penates*, spirits of household prosperity, were linked to ancestors, and wax figures of them were made and placed in special shrines in the home.

druid ancestors

The spirits of the ancestors are specifically venerated in the Druid tradition, which draws on ancient practices, making them relevant to modern pagans. The term 'Druid' is used very loosely, for it is unclear exactly who the Druids were, for they left no written records. What we do know is that the ancient Britons buried their dead in sacred sites, often arranging their bones with symbolic meanings and returning to the chambered barrow-mounds to commune and worship. The world of the ancestors was a treasure house of radiant wisdom.

Today, we are especially conscious of rebelling against the repressive teachings of our parents, but that does not mean we cannot honour what is good, wise and enriching from our heritage. In pagan ritual, the west is the home of the Islands of the Blessed where the dead go to rest between incarnations, and rites that venerate those who have passed may be performed facing west.

venerating genetic inheritance

Some of us find it hard to respect what has been handed down to us from our parents, and this will be especially true if you have been badly treated or come from a dogmatic and harsh background. However, honouring the ancestors is not about following specific beliefs or trying to force yourself to feel warmly towards those who have damaged you. It is about venerating your genetic inheritance, the wisdom within your blood and bones, and all the wondrous legacy of past incarnations. It means putting down roots for your spiritual growth.

The ancestors are venerated in many ways in China, giving a reassuring sense of continuity. They are ever-present for the living.

an altar to the ancestors

Creating an altar to your ancestors is a good way to honour your genetic inheritance, but perhaps it would be helpful to establish what should not go on your altar! Sepia photos of relatives who mean nothing to you, pictures of those that you did not respect and heirlooms that you dislike are not true reminders of your ancestry. Guilt and duty have nothing to do with this altar, and if your immediate ancestors do not inspire you, then look farther back. There must have been plenty who were good to make the spiritual seeker that you are today.

Choose the images for your ancestral altar with care. The purpose is to connect with something meaningful.

Think about some of your best qualities – maybe courage, creativity or a healing touch. What have you heard about your family history that might be connected with these qualities? Maybe several generations ago you had an ancestor who was a celebrated painter or poet, or perhaps you had a great-great aunt who was a nurse in a war. Researching your family tree may help turn up some information, but detailed information isn't necessary – it is spiritual heritage that counts. If you have a picture of an ancestor to whom you are especially drawn, then give that person pride of place on your altar, bringing to that image flowers and lighting a candle on special occasions. Ask that person to be with you when you need inspiration in life and see what happens.

borrow from other cultures

You can adapt some traditions from other cultures to help with your ancestor altar. You can obtain clay that hardens without firing, make this into a tablet and engrave it with anything you feel is significant – possibly a family motto, a name, or even a saying from a culture you link with your guide, such as Native American or Chinese wisdom. Go with what is meaningful to you.

Draw on Druid tradition by placing your ancestor altar in the west. Burn oil of rosemary for remembrance or myrrh. Tend your altar as the Sun goes down, realizing that as you look at the sunset you are gazing at your own past and your future, as the old gives way to the new in a constant cycle.

Bring regular offerings to your altar. The Roman habit of honouring the *Lares* with a garland is a beautiful one, especially if you have made it yourself from your own garden. As with your fairy altar, offerings of food and drink can be placed there temporarily, before you place them outside.

affirming a connection

If you have a strong sense of a guide from a previous incarnation, then you may wish to affirm this connection on your altar, by effigies and other appropriate artefacts. For instance, if your guide is Chinese, a jade figure would be apt; if he is Egyptian, then you might prefer an Egyptian statue that strikes the right note for you. When contact with your guide is established, he or she may suggest things and they might be quite amusing!

making an ancestor collage

The basic guidelines for making an ancestor collage are the same that you employ for making an ancestor altar – use nothing that makes you feel resentful or bad in any way. Place no one's picture on your collage until you feel that it should be included. When you look at your collage, it should convey to you the pattern of your ancestral and guide experience and communication. It will remind you of your achievements and inspire you.

An ancestral collage can be fascinating! It is an absorbing way to become involved with your spiritual heritage.

getting started

1 Gather your materials and let your intuition and imagination go. You might like to start your collage with a picture of the setting sun on the left (west as it would appear on a map) and one of the rising sun on the right (east).

2 Think about your talents and achievements. If you have children, this will probably include them. Place representations of these fairly centrally in your collage, (although children, as the future, should perhaps be towards the east). Also place any examples of your creativity, such as a poem you have written or something you have drawn. Postcards of significant places that you have visited, pieces of fabric from an important garment, ribbons of a significant colour, dried leaves and flowers, feathers – all these can play a part. You might like to include a photograph of yourself.

3 Around the sunset corner, group the past, including photos of ancestors who have had a positive effect, whose attributes you value or who offer you guidance.

4 In the rising sun corner, place tokens of what you wish to achieve, especially spiritually; include symbolic portraits such as a dove, an angel or a star. If you want more concrete things, such as a new career, use symbols to represent what you want. Keep away from anything too specific. This is about your spiritual journey, so choose with that in mind or your collage will have a limited shelf-life.

5 For the rest of the collage, move towards what is more explicitly spiritual, towards your individual spirit guide. He or she may well be working with ancestral spirits (as well as angels, fairies and power animals) but he or she is also a vibrant part of your past, perhaps in a previous life. In the lower part of the collage, place representations of what you know, sense or believe was your past life with this guide. For instance, if this seems to you to have been in ancient Egypt, this is the place for Egyptian pictures and symbols.

6 In the upper part of the collage, place representations of more current and developing themes – maybe experiences you have had of your guide or places where you have felt him close. For instance, if you were walking somewhere and your guide seemed to 'speak' to you, a daisy that you picked at that time could be dried, pressed and added to the collage. You may like to leave space to add more items, as you progress.

a meditation to meet your guide

This meditation is intended to pave the way for you to meet and commune with your own special spirit guide. It follows on from the visualization on pages 24–25 that prepares you to draw close to your spirit guide. If you have time, prepare for it beforehand (see pages 20–21) so that your state of mind is calm and a little detached. Relax as explained on pages 22–23.

meeting your guide meditation

Before you begin, think first about the words that you will use to ask your guide to approach you; this could be in the form of a short invocation or just a simple line.

1 Imagine that you are facing the doorway or archway that formed part of your preliminary ritual (see page 19). Go through the opening and find yourself on the path. You might like to take a fairy of the elements, your power animal or an angelic being with you for support. However, there is no need to overcrowd your path – just have with you those beings with whom you feel an affinity.

2 When you reach the plateau, go towards the lake and wash your face and hands in its crystal waters. Feel the air fresh upon your skin. Look around you, noticing the flowers and rocks, and the shape of your own astral temple within easy walking distance. Look now towards the rainbow bridge, to where it makes contact with the meadow, shimmering and glistening. Walk towards the rainbow bridge and step within its radiance.

3 Sense a gentle tingling all over your body and feel
   wonderfully uplifted. You may hear sounds or be
   aware of other presences. Ask for your guide to come
   to you, using the words or invocation that you have
   prepared. Soon you will be aware of a gentle and wise
   presence within the rainbow light. You may see an
   actual figure, you may smell a scent or simply feel that
   he or she is there. Now ask for a signal; ask for it three
   times to establish that this is your true guide.

4 You may now walk with your guide to your astral
   temple to commune further or stay where you are.
   Ask the name of your guide – don't worry if you get
   no clear answer, for this will probably come in the
   ensuing weeks. If there is something on your mind,
   speak with your guide about it, but do not expect
   too much, as this is a first contact.

5 After a short while, take leave of your guide, saying
   'thank you' and promising to return. Follow the path
   back with any helpers you have with you. Take
   respectful leave of them too, and return through your
   doorway. Bring yourself back to the here and now by
   patting your body, eating and drinking something and
   recording all you have experienced in your diary.

GROWING WITH YOUR SPIRIT GUIDE

Now that you have made contact with your guides, you may wish to strengthen the links and take things further. If your rapport with your guide is good, you will be shown what to do and will be able to go forward in a manner that is best suited to you. If you still do not feel confident that you are in communication with a true guide, then please revisit the exercises at the beginning of the book and be patient. If you are a sincere seeker, in time you will achieve what you want.

Once in good contact with your spirit guides, you will need few instructions from anywhere else, but some hints are always handy – in fact. your guides will help to connect you with people and with information that can help you. The following short chapter gives you some pointers on how you might like to develop.

The modern phenomenon of 'channelling' can enable you to receive messages from your guide in a state of consciousness that is closer to the everyday awareness than when you are in deep meditation. Some people become quite talented at this and may be able to 'receive' messages that are helpful to others, although such messages need to be assessed carefully. In dreams, we travel into other worlds and by becoming more aware of this, vivid contact may be made with guides. Finally, there are plenty of groups of like-minded people that you can join, to explore further.

Go forward and be blessed.

channelling

'Channelling' means acting as a channel for spiritual wisdom. Good channelling will almost always come from one source, through a personal guide. Of course, whenever you interact with a guide you are 'channelling' in a way, but such messages do not come directly into the everyday world. When you channel, you are in this world.

Make yourself comfortable and allow yourself to relax before attempting channelling. In this way the images will flow more easily.

how to channel

Channelling means going into a relaxed and slightly different level of consciousness, like day-dreaming, except that you are focused and using control and direction. Before channelling, protect yourself by donning a cloak of light (see pages 26–27) and asking for protective spirits such as your power animal to be present, since you are laying yourself open.

Settle yourself somewhere peaceful and safe, where you will not be interrupted. Allow yourself to feel dreamy and open, and see what comes into your mind. If you have a question, formulate this clearly before commencing – then 'let go' of the question and let the images flow. Messages may come verbally, as symbols, pictures, scents or bodily feelings. If you hold a pen lightly over a sheet of paper, you may feel you want to write. If you are a musician, you may want to play a tune, and if you are artistic, you may feel inspired to paint. It may seem natural to you to speak aloud, and if your state of consciousness is removed from the everyday, it will be a good idea to have a tape-recorder running so you have a record.

channelling for other people

If you become good at channelling, you may be able to do this for other people and your guide may encourage this. However, this is an area that requires tremendous care. What comes through when you or anyone else channels is coloured by the views and beliefs of the person channelling. If someone else channels for you, be aware of the following:

- Despite the possible glamour and/or confidence of the person channelling, is he or she in contact with a truly wise spirit?
- Spirits can be boring, misleading, mischievous and plain wrong! Never suspend common sense.
- Is the channeller reasonably well balanced? Psychic abilities are not an indication of true spirituality and it is possible to be greatly gifted and deeply misguided, as well as plain nasty or even mentally unstable.
- No true guidance will ever be dogmatic, threatening, controlling or judgemental. If it makes you feel bad, then it's bad guidance.

Remember the pointers when you channel for yourself. Keep a relaxed attitude, with humour and reverence combined. As time goes by you will recognize what is important. You may also realize that you have, in your creativity, been 'channelling' all along and with awareness this will grow.

dreamwork

Every night we spend many hours in another world – the world of the subconscious mind. It can be useful and workable to regard the subconscious as very close to the realm of the Otherworld. It is well known that many people have received 'messages' in dreams, that dreams can foretell the future and bring inspiration. Some people believe they can contact those who have died in their dreams, and your dreams are one avenue that your spirit guide may be able to use to communicate with you.

Some people assert that they never dream, but this is most unlikely to be the case. We all dream but not all of us can remember our dreams – this can be encouraged by correct habits and some mental training. Firstly, get into the habit of jotting down your dreams as soon as you wake up. This does not have to be anything lengthy – just by writing something you are sending a message to your subconscious that you are taking note and more will be delivered.

Writing down your dreams affirms to your subconscious that you are taking note of its messages. In this way dreams may be encouraged.

herbal aids to dreamwork

According to folklore, there are many herbs that can aid dreams:

- *To encourage wise dreams, place ash or bay leaves, or an onion or peppermint leaves, under your pillow.*

- *A tea made of rosebuds, sipped before sleeping, is a sweeter alternative.*

- *Jasmine oil heated in a diffuser in the bedroom will encourage you to have revealing dreams, and golden marigolds under the bed have a similar effect.*

- *Mimosa may also be placed under the pillow or the pillow itself may be stuffed with mugwort.*

learning to recall your dreams

If you cannot remember any dreams, change your sleeping routine. Devote time and attention to preparing for bed, rather than falling asleep in front of the television or crashing exhausted on to your pillow. Make sure that your bed is really comfortable and the temperature of the bedroom just right. Have a bed-time ritual: take a relaxing bath, read a poem or two, light a candle or update your personal journal. Affirm that you are going to sleep well and dream important dreams. Go to bed a little earlier, to change your rhythms, or set the alarm half an hour earlier to break your sleep at a point where you can 'catch' your dreams.

Most important of all, ask your guide to communicate with you in your dreams and to show you ways to remember them. If you have any symbols or substances that you associate with your guide, place them by your bed.

crystal dreams

Crystals also can help you recall your dreams, and one of the loveliest crystals for this is amethyst. If you can obtain a sizeable piece of amethyst or even a geode, place this beside your bed to have spiritual and uplifting dreams. Rhodochrosite brings creative dreams while celestite, green sapphire and jasper all aid dream recall. In fact, any crystal that makes you feel peaceful and uplifted can only help in the process.

working in groups

Group working can be very helpful, as long as it is the right group, and as long as you come to it with the right attitude. Do not search for a guru or expect to have all your questions answered for you. Group leaders are often leaders because of their leadership ability, not because they have special spiritual powers.

Many people want to be given firm guidance and it may be comforting to have a leader telling you what to do. However, remember firstly that, the map is not the country! The tools and practices to which your group leader may introduce you can help you navigate the subtle realms and give you an anchor, but they are not going to be the last word on the matter. Secondly, while it is important to be tolerant of your group leader, do not tolerate being disempowered. You should never be made to feel small, stupid or 'unspiritual'.

where to look for a group

A group that answers your needs may be found through advertisements, especially in New Age shops or similar. Take the time to explore and enquire – personal recommendation is always best. Shamanic lodges will help you connect with your power animal and workshops on angels, fairies and spirit guides can also be found.

how they work

In all probability you will be guided through visualizations similar to those in this book, and it is wonderful to be helped in this way and to have other people with whom to discuss what you have experienced. What others encounter may have a synchronicity with you, and all of you may achieve greater clarity as a result. Occasionally someone will have a 'message' for you, and this may be very helpful (but see the pointers to watch for in the

A carefully chosen group can be a great help in spiritual development because it offers support and encouragement.

previous pages). Of course, any group you join does not have to be specifically concerned with contacting guides – you may find help and kindred spirits in Wiccan and astrological groups, or those concerned with tarot, crystals, channelling and many others.

preparing to attend a group

When attending a group for the first time, place your cloak of light around yourself (see pages 26–27), and let this grow until if forms a protective egg around your body. This egg has a membrane – it lets out your good wishes and it lets in benevolence from others, but nothing harmful can penetrate its shining circumference. Imagine this and affirm it. See any negative influences bouncing off it and falling to the ground to be neutralized. If you have already made sound contact with your guide, he or she will give you advice about the group. Do not make yourself vulnerable in any way until you are sure you can trust your companions.

With any luck you will be able to form a connection with other seekers who will journey with you and be a valuable support.

index

acknowledgements

Executive Editor Sandra Rigby
Editor Ruth Wiseall
Executive Art Editor Penny Stock
Designer Barbara Zuñiga
Photographer Russell Sadur
Senior Production Controller Simone Nauerth

Special Photography © Octopus Publishing Group Ltd/Russell Sadur

Other Photography Alamy/David Gee 111; /Elizabeth Whiting and
Associates 71; /Jason Lindsay 29; /Juniors Bildarchiv 13; /Jupiterimages 90;
/Loetscher Martin 94; /The Photolibrary Wales 97. Bridgeman Art
Library/Louvre, Paris, France 32; /Pinacoteca di Brera, Milan, Italy, 35; 64.
Corbis UK Ltd/A Green 59; Buddy Mays 70; Bruno Ehrs 108. Getty Images
88; /Hulton Archive 33; /Martin Harvey 25. istockphoto.com 24; /Ana Abejon
26; /Serdar Uckun 95. Mary Evans Picture Library 62; 92. Octopus Publishing
Group Limited 37, 38, 38, 39, 39, 39, 40, 40, 41, 41, 41, 43, 49, 83, 99, 122,
125, 17, 38, 49; /Ruth Jenkinson 14, 27 43; /Russell Sadur 16, 20 21, 99, 120,
123, 125. Photolibrary Ian Oleary 60. Shutterstock 12, 36, 46, 72; 74, 79; 96.
Sothebys 66. The Art Archive Biblioteca Nazionale Marciana Venice/Gianni
Dagli Orti 11. TopFoto/Fortean 91.